WHAT WAS MARK AT?

Wilfrid J. Harrington, O.P.

What was Mark at?
The Gospel of Mark: A Commentary

the columba press

First published, 2008, by
the columba press
55A Spruce Avenue, Stillorgan Industrial Park,
Blackrock, Co Dublin

Cover by Bill Bolger
Origination by The Columba Press
Printed in Ireland by Colour Books Ltd, Dublin

ISBN 978 1 85607 634 0

Contents

Preface

A gospel is a Christian document addressed to Christians. All four evangelists were concerned to set out both the story of Jesus and also what they took to be the significance of his actions and teaching. In practice, each gospel was written for a particular Christian community and with the needs of that community firmly in mind.

Today, when we as Christians begin to read a gospel, we already know the lines of the story. The first readers or hearers of each gospel already knew the Jesus story as well as the evangelist. Each evangelist put a 'spin' on a familiar story. The reader will ask: why is he telling the story like this? In telling the story in his specific manner, each evangelist has written a literary text. One of the joys of studying the gospels is a growing appreciation of the literary sophistication of the evangelists. One repeatedly discovers something fresh to admire.

Mark's is the earliest of the gospels. It is a taut text. Behind the text is a brilliant storyteller and a thoughtful theologian. Increasingly, Mark has become my favourite gospel. I believe I admire most the evangelist's realism. It confirms my conviction that the cross is indeed the heart of Christianity – the heart as understood by Paul and Mark and the author of Revelation. Mark's theology is a theology of the cross and Mark's Jesus is the most human in the gospels.

The gospel according to Mark sets the pattern of a gospel: it is concerned with christology (the theological understanding of Jesus) and discipleship. Jesus is the Son of God. He is Son of Man – the one come to serve, the one faithful unto death. A person who has come to terms with the cross (with the meaning of his death) can know him and confess him – like the centurion (Mk 15: 39). His disciples did not understand him before Calvary. The Christian reader of the first century and of today is being challenged to come to terms with the love of God shown forth in the cross of Christ.

Wilfrid J. Harrington OP

Introduction

Mark: The Triumph of Failure
Underestimated from early times because of its brevity (almost all of Mark is found in Matthew and Luke), the gospel of Mark has, in our day, come into its own Above all, the evangelist Mark stands side-by-side with Paul as a stalwart proclaimer of a *theologia crucis* – a theology of the cross. And, congenial to modern christology, the Marcan Jesus is the most human in the gospels. The gospel according to Mark sets the pattern of a gospel: it is concerned with christology and discipleship. Jesus is the Son of God, that is, God-appointed leader of the renewed covenant people; he is 'son of man', the human one come to serve, the one faithful unto death. A person who has come to terms with the cross (with the meaning of his death) can know him and confess him – like the centurion (Mk 13: 39). His disciples did not understand him before Calvary. The Christian reader of the first century, and of today, is being challenged to come to terms with the love of God shown forth in the cross of Jesus.

The Setting of Mark
The view that Mark had written in Rome about 65AD and for people in Rome, had long been the prevalent one. But it has not gone unchallenged, because the traditional data that point to this provenance and date are of uncertain worth. We are forced back to the text of the gospel: to an anonymous writing of the first Christian century. The author is not named in the gospel; the traditional name 'Mark' was quite common. Nothing in the gospel points necessarily to a Roman origin. We can be sure that 'Mark' wrote for a specific community and in the face of the actual circumstances of that community. We are left to tease out a plausible setting for his gospel and its likely date.

Today we confidently set the writing of the gospel close to the events of the Jewish war of 66-70AD. A careful reading of Mark 13 would suggest a date soon after the Roman destruction of Jerusalem in 70AD. Together with mounting scholarly opinion, I would propose that Mark was written to and for a Christian community somewhere in the province of Syria. This would offer a setting close to the tragic events of the war. The community may even have harboured Christian refugees from the conflict, making it that more immediate.

The gospel of Mark, after an introduction (1: 1-13) which sets the stage for the drama to follow, is built up of two complementary parts. The first (1:14–8:30) is concerned with the mystery of Jesus' identity: it is dominated by the question 'Who is Jesus?' The emphasis in this part of Mark is on Jesus' miracles; the teaching is largely parabolic. The second part (8: 31–15: 47) is concerned with the messianic destiny of Jesus: a way of suffering and death. The emphasis in this second half of Mark is on Jesus' teaching which, now directed at his disciples, builds upon their acknowledgment of him as Messiah. It is concerned mainly with the nature of his messiahship and with the suffering it will entail both for himself and for his followers.

The Gospel and the Man
'Who then is this?' (4:41). The question was wrung from the awestruck disciples of Jesus when, at his word, a great calm had fallen upon the troubled waters and their storm-tossed boat had come to rest. For Mark, that chastened crew might have been the community, the little church, for which he wrote. He wrote for people such as those who needed to know Jesus, who wanted to understand who he really was. He wrote for Christians who doubted and were fearful: 'Teacher, do you not care if we perish?' (v 38). He wrote for Christians who did not relish the idea of being disciples of a suffering Messiah. He wrote for Christians very like ourselves. His gospel is as tract for our time.

We may ask, what of Mark? His gospel shows him to be a storyteller of great natural talent, a man with an eye for telling detail, a man who could effectively structure his material. Mark emerges, too, as a theologian of stature. Some have argued for a Pauline influence on Mark. Whatever of that, the Christ of Mark is a Christ whom Paul would recognise, and the gospel of Mark is one that Paul would not have disdained to call his own. Mark's gospel is the gospel of Jesus Christ, the 'Son of God' and closes with the resounding declaration: 'Truly, this man was God's Son!' And yet, his Jesus is a man who was indignant and angry, who took children into his arms, a man who suffered and died. This Son of Man who came 'not to be served but to serve, and to give his life as a ransom for many' (10:45) is the Christ whom Paul preached: 'When I came to you, brothers and sisters, I did not come proclaiming the mystery of God to you in lofty words or wisdom. For I decided to know nothing among you except Jesus Christ and him crucified' (1 Cor 2: 1-2). Paul the Apostle, the first great Christian theologian, had come to terms with the scandal of the cross. Mark the evangelist is, perhaps, the next notable Christian theologian in line.

The Triumph of Failure

In human culture, victory is celebrated. We are aware of the significance of winning in sport. It is often remarked that no one remembers who came second in an Olympic event. We need, sympathetically, to appreciate the challenge to our earliest brothers and sisters, who had, in a context of Jewish messianic hope, first of all to accept, and then to market, the Christian gospel. Because, at first sight, by human standards, Jesus was a tragic failure. Paul, the Jew, was keenly aware of the problem: 'We proclaim Christ crucified, a stumbling block to Jews and foolishness to Gentiles, but to those who are called, both Jews and Greeks, Christ the power of God and the wisdom of God' (1 Cor 2: 23-24). Jewish expectation looked to a triumphalist Davidic Messiah. Peter's reaction at Caesarea Philippi is wholly understandable (Mk 8: 32). He had declared Jesus to be Messiah – and Jesus had gone on to speak of rejection and death! It was, for Peter, a contradiction in terms.

The reality: Jesus was indeed the Messiah who was rejected and crucified. Given that dominant Jewish expectation, typically represented by Peter, it is indeed remarkable that Jesus is so firmly proclaimed as Messiah across the New Testament traditions. His designation, Jesus Christ, with 'Christ' almost as a second name, is, in effect, confession of his messiahship: *Iésous Christos*, Jesus, the Messiah.

As in story generally, the events and action of the Marcan story involve conflict, and Jesus is the immediate cause of the conflict. We may illustrate by glancing, firstly, at conflicts between Jesus and the authorities, and then at those between Jesus and his disciples.

Jesus versus the authorities

The authorities involved were the religious and political leaders and in relation to them Jesus was at a disadvantage. Mark does indeed show Jesus having facile authority over evil spirits – the exorcisms, and over nature – the stilling of the storm. But Jesus' authority did not extend to lording it over people. Still, what Jesus said and did challenged directly the authorities of Israel. For their part these authorities viewed themselves as defenders of God's law. They contended that Jesus assumed unwarranted legal authority for himself, interpreted the law in a manner they considered illegal, and disregarded many religious customs. They responded by uttering charges against him.

Jesus, for his part, had been anointed to usher in God's rule (1: 9-11). The issue for him was how to get the authorities to 'see' God's authority in his actions and teaching. The narrator skilfully created tension and suspense. By the end of the five conflict-stories (2:1–3:6) the sides are clearly established (3:6). The impending clash with the authorities is kept in sight during the journey to Jerusalem (2:27–10:52). The climactic confrontation in Jerusalem came quickly. It is noteworthy that the first accusation against Jesus was a charge of blasphemy: 'Why does this man speak in this way? It is blasphemy!' (2:7) – thus, from the start of the story Jesus walks a tightrope. Nevertheless, the reader recognises that Jesus is firmly in control. At the trial he himself volunteered the evidence his accusers needed. 'Are you the Messiah, the Son of the Blessed One?' Jesus answered, 'I am' (14: 61-62). Jesus, not the authorities, determined his fate.

The narrator resolves the conflict with the authorities only when they condemned Jesus and put him to death. It was an ironic resolution. The authorities had, unwittingly, co-operated in bringing to pass God's purpose. By means of this ironic resolution, the story depicts Jesus as the real authority in Israel. The authorities condemned as blasphemy Jesus' claim to be Son of God but, since in the story world Jesus' claim is true, they are the ones guilty of blasphemy. The irony is hidden from the authorities, but it is not hidden from the reader. The reader knows that Jesus will be established in power and the authorities condemned (8:28–9:1; 13: 24-27, 30-32; 14: 62).

Jesus and the disciples

At stake in the conflict with the disciples is whether Jesus can make them good disciples. The disciples struggled at every point to follow Jesus but were simply overwhelmed both by him and his demands. Jesus' efforts to lead the disciples to understand were matched by their fear and their hardness of heart. Theirs was not the determined opposition to Jesus of the authorities – they were trying to be his followers. They did consistently misunderstand Jesus' teaching and ended up by failing him utterly. Yet, they had followed him to Jerusalem. Jesus just could not lead his chosen disciples (effectively, the Twelve) to understand him, could not get them to do what he expected of them. In an effort to bring them to realise how dense and blind they were, he hurled challenging questions at them (4:13, 40; 8:17-21, 33; 9:19; 14:37, 41), and was met with silence. He tried to prepare them for his impending death and for his absence. He knew that they would fail him in Jerusalem; yet he sought to urge them to stand by him (14:37, 41-42). The outer conflict reflects an inner conflict: they want to be loyal to Jesus, but not at the cost of giving up everything, least of all their lives. The fact remains that readers of the gospel are most likely to empathise with those same disciples. By doing so the readers come to discern their own inadequacies. They find comfort in the realisation that, although the disciples failed him, Jesus remained unflinchingly faithful to them.

Jesus did not, however, manage to make them faithful disciples. They failed him – and the question stands: will they learn from their failure and, beyond his death, at last become true followers of him? When Jesus had warned his disciples of their impending failure (14: 26-31) he had added a reassuring word: 'After I am raised up, I will go before you to Galilee' (14:28). That word is then caught up in the message of the 'young man' at the tomb: 'Go, tell his disciples and Peter that he is going before you to Galilee; there you will see him, just as he told you' (16:7). Throughout the gospel 'to see' Jesus means to have faith in him. What Mark is saying is that if the community is to 'see' Jesus, now the Risen One, it must become involved in the mission to the world that 'Galilee' signified. Galilee was the place of mission, the arena where Jesus' exorcisms and healings had broken the bonds of evil. There, too, the disciples had been called and commissioned to take up Jesus' proclamation of the coming rule of God. 'Galilee' is the place of universal mission. But no disciple is ready to proclaim the gospel until she or he has walked the way to Jerusalem (10: 32-34) and encountered the reality of the cross.

The minor characters

The narrator shows the authorities in a consistently negative light. The disciples are shown in an unflattering light. In contrast, the characterisation of the minor characters is firmly positive. Here, indeed, is an eye-opener. One's attention is drawn to something so obvious that it had escaped our attention. The fact is that, over against both opponents and disciples, minor characters in the gospel steadfastly exemplify the values of the rule of God. Mark seems to be reminding his community that the sterling Christian qualities are to be found in the 'simple faithful'.

The narrator developed these 'little people' as foils to the authorities and disciples and as parallels to Jesus. These minor characters do measure up to Jesus' standards – especially as they exemplify the values of faith, of being least, of willingness to serve. In the first half of the gospel they measure up to Jesus' opening summons: 'Be converted, and believe in the good news' (for example, 1:29-31, 40-45; 5: 18-20, 21-43; 7:24-30, 31-27; 8:22-27). In the final scenes, in Jerusalem, the minor characters exemplify especially the teaching about being 'servant of all'. Where, before, Jesus had served others, in his time of need others served him. The consistent conduct of the 'little people' stands in sharp contrast to the conduct of the Twelve. In the first half of the story, while there is no direct comparison, the minor characters emerge as models of faith – more than could be said of the Twelve. In the last scenes in Jerusalem the minor characters do fulfil the functions expected of disciples. Here the 'little people' are highlighted (10:46-52; 14:3-9; 15:40-41; 16:1-8).

Henceforth, any enlightened reading of Mark's gospel must acknowledge the major contribution of its minor characters.

Failure

Mark was keenly aware of the paradox at the heart of Christianity, a paradox dramatically presented by the author of Revelation: the Victim is the Victor. The story of Jesus, as told in Mark, is a story of human failure: the failure of Israel, the failure of the disciples, the seeming failure of Jesus himself. Yet, Jesus, the Son, won through to 'resurrection life' by his openness to the ways of God. Faithfulness to God led him to acceptance of death on the cross, thereby becoming Messiah and Son of God. In his mission Jesus sought to draw others into a following of this way. Failure of the disciples reached its climax in their flight at the arrest of Jesus (14:50). It seemed that women disciples had redeemed the situation. They, albeit at a distance, witnessed the crucifixion (15:40), saw where the body had been laid (15:47) and, later, came to anoint it (16:1). Assured that Jesus had been raised (16:6) they were commanded to take the Easter message to the failed disciples (16:70). Mark has the last, unexpected, word: 'So they went out and fled from the tomb, for terror and amazement seized them; and they said nothing to any one, for they were afraid' (16:8). At the last the women join the men disciples in failure, sharing their fear and flight.

In the end, all humans fail. God alone succeeds. The Father had not abandoned the Son (15:34) but had raised Jesus from the dead (16:6). The failed disciples will encounter the risen Lord in Galilee (14:28; 16:7). Not because they have succeeded, but solely because of the initiative of God. Fulfilment of the promise of 14:28, 16:7 is not in the text of Mark's gospel. It is in the Christian community that received the story.

> The conclusion of Mark's gospel is not a message of failure but a resounding affirmation of God's design to overcome all imaginable failure (16:1-8) in and through the action of God's beloved Son (1:1-13). The words addressed to the struggling disciples at the Transfiguration are addressed to all who take up this gospel: 'Listen to him' (9:7). (Francis J. Moloney, *The Gospel of Mark. A Commentary*, Peabody, MA: Hendrickson, 2002, p 354).

Plan of the Gospel

PART I: THE MYSTERY OF THE MESSIAH

Prologue 1: 1- 13

Revelation of Jesus' Person 1: 14 – 8:30
Three sections, each *beginning* with a summary of the
activity of Jesus and a narrative concerning the disciples,
and *concluding* with the adoption of an attitude in regard to
Jesus:
A. Jesus Welcomed and Challenged 1:14–3: 6
(1:14-15, 16-20; 3:6)
B. He Came to His Own 3:7–6:6a
(3:7-12, 13-16; 6:1-6a)
C. Jesus and the Disciples 6: 6b–8: 30
(6:6b, 7-31; 8:27-30)

Conclusion and Transition: Who is Jesus? 8: 27-33

PART II: THE MYSTERY OF THE SON OF MAN

Revelation of Jesus' Suffering 8:3 –15:47

A. The Way of the Son of Man 8:31-10:52
Signposted by three announcements of the fate of the Son of
Man leading to three instructions on the way of discipleship.

B. Jesus in Jerusalem 11:1–13:37

C. The Passion of Jesus 14: –15:47

Epilogue 16: 1-8

The Commentary

Prologue 1:1–13

¹The beginning of the good news of Jesus Christ, the Son of God.
²As it is written in the prophet Isaiah,
>'See, I am sending my messenger ahead of you,
>who will prepare your way;
>³the voice of one crying out in the wilderness:
>"Prepare the way of the Lord, make his paths straight".'

⁴John the baptiser appeared in the wilderness, proclaiming a baptism of repentance for the forgiveness of sins. ⁵And people from the whole Judean countryside and all the people of Jerusalem were going out to him, and were baptised by him in the river Jordan, confessing their sins. ⁶Now John was clothed with camel's hair, with a leather belt around his waist, and he ate locusts and wild honey. ⁷He proclaimed, 'The one who is more powerful than I is coming after me; I am not worthy to stoop down and untie the thong of his sandals. ⁸I have baptised you with water; but he will baptise you with the Holy Spirit.'

⁹In those days Jesus came from Nazareth of Galilee and was baptised by John in the Jordan. ¹⁰And just as he was coming up out of the water, he saw the heavens torn apart and the Spirit descending like a dove on him. ¹¹And a voice came from heaven, 'You are my Son, the Beloved; with you I am well pleased.'

¹²And the Spirit immediately drove him out into the wilderness. ¹³He was in the wilderness forty days, tempted by Satan; and he was with the wild beasts; and the angels waited on him.

The caption of this gospel – 'The beginning of the good news of Jesus Christ, the Son of God' – informs the reader of Mark's own understanding of Jesus' identity. The beginning and abiding source of the gospel lies in the historical appearance of Jesus who, in the perspective of the Easter faith of the church, was recognisable as Son of God. As in each of the gospels, the Christian reader is, at the very start, told clearly and firmly who Jesus is.

The good news centred on Jesus Christ opens with the emergence of the wilderness prophet John, clothed like Elijah (2 Kings 1:8) and subsisting on wilderness fare. While it is likely that the Baptist proclaimed imminent judgement – 'baptism with fire' (see Mt 3:11; Lk

3:16) – here his message is transformed into a prophecy of the out-pouring of the Spirit, a work of the risen Lord. In Mark neither John nor Jesus preach judgement.

The Forerunner had made his solemn proclamation: we await the emergence of the Coming One. Jesus came from Nazareth of Galilee to be baptised by John. According to Mark, at the baptism, the heav-enly voice (the voice of God) declared of Jesus: 'You are my Son, the Beloved.' As Jesus was about to embark on his public mission, God solemnly approved both his status and his call. Similarly, at the transfiguration, God declared (this time for the benefit of the three disciples), 'This is my Son, the Beloved; listen to him!' (9:7). Only at baptism and transfiguration does God emerge as 'actor' in the story. And not alone did God, each time, declare that Jesus was 'Son', but the declaration served the purpose of confirmation. The baptism declaration confirmed the truth of the caption (1:1); the transfiguration declaration confirmed the truth of Peter's confes-sion of Jesus as the 'Messiah' (8:29).

Jesus was constituted and declared Son of God at the moment of his baptism by John. A new era had begun, the era of God's reign. It must entail the overthrow of evil, personified as Satan. This Mark conveys by combining the temptation narrative (vv 12-13) with the baptism narrative (vv 9-11). He has managed, too, a striking con-trast in his presentation of Forerunner and Coming One. John is a man among crowds, preaching and baptising. With the appearance of Jesus we enter another world: the heavens torn open, the Spirit descending, a divine Voice, the Son of God, the power of the Spirit, Satan tempting, ministering angels.

Jesus was tempted. The Greek word carries all the nuances of tempt-ation, trial, tribulation, test. For Jesus, temptation did not end here (see 14:32-42), and the implied victory over Satan, reflected in his subsequent exorcisms, will have to be won all over again on the cross. Here we are doubtless to understand that the ministering angels supplied Jesus with food; Mark has no suggestion at all of a fast of Jesus. At this struggle Jesus does not feel God-forsaken as he will feel at his last (15:34).

A. Jesus Welcomed and Challenged 1:14–3:6

The Mission Begins 1:14-45

[14]Now after John was **arrested** [delivered up], Jesus came to Galilee, proclaiming the good news of God, [15]and saying, 'The time is fulfilled, and the kingdom of God has come near; repent and believe in the good news.'

[16]As Jesus passed along the sea of Galilee, he saw Simon and his brother Andrew casting a net into the sea – for they were fishermen. [17]And Jesus said to them, 'Follow me and I will make you fish for people.' [18]And immediately they left their nets, and followed him. [19]As he went a little farther, he saw James son of Zebedee and his brother John, who were in their boat mending the nets. [20]Immediately he called them; and they left their father Zebedee in the boat with the hired men, and followed him.

[21]They went to Capernaum; and when the Sabbath came, he entered the synagogue and taught. [22]They were astounded at his teaching, for he taught them as one having authority, and not as the scribes. [23]Just then there was in their synagogue a man with an unclean spirit. [24]And he cried out, 'What have you to do with us, Jesus of Nazareth? Have you come to destroy us? I know who you are, the Holy One of God.' [25]But Jesus rebuked him, saying, 'Be silent, and come out of him!' [26]And the unclean spirit, convulsing him and crying out with a loud voice, came out of him. [27]And they were all amazed, and they kept on asking one another, 'What is this? A new teaching – with authority! He commands even the unclean spirits, and they obey him.' [28]At once his fame began to spreads throughout the surrounding region of Galilee.

[29]As soon as they left the synagogue, they entered the house of Simon and Andrew, with James and John [30]Now Simon's mother-in-law was in bed with a fever, and they told him about her at once. [31]He came and took her by the hand and lifted her up. Then the fever left her, and she began to serve them.

[32]That evening, at sundown, they brought to him all who were sick or possessed with demons. [33]And the whole city was gathered around the door. [34]And he cured many who were sick with various diseases, and cast out many demons; and he would not permit the demons to speak, because they knew him.

[35]In the morning, while it was still very dark, he got up and went out to a deserted place, and there he prayed. [36]And Simon and his companions hunted for him. [37]When they found him they said to

him, 'Everyone is searching for you.' [38]He answered, 'Let us go on to the neighbouring towns, so that I may proclaim the message there also; for that is what I came out to do.' [39]And he went throughout Galilee, proclaiming the message in their synagogues and casting out demons.

[40]A leper came to him begging him, and kneeling he said to him, 'If you choose, you can make me clean.' [41]Moved with anger [pity], Jesus stretched out his hand and touched him, and said to him, 'I do choose. Be made clean!' [42]Immediately the leprosy left him, and he was made clean. [43]After sternly warning him he sent him away at once, [44]saying to him, 'See that you say nothing to anyone; but go, show yourself to the priest, and offer for your cleansing what Moses commanded, as a testimony to them.' [45]But he went out and began to proclaim it freely, and to repeat the word, so that Jesus could no longer go into a town openly, but stayed out in the country; and people came to him from every quarter.

Now that Jesus has been acknowledged as God's Son, and has thrown himself into a totally committed struggle against evil, he can begin to preach the good news. Mark's first summary statement (1:14-15) – summary statements are a feature of his style – opens the mission of Jesus and covers its initial stage. The opening words, however, are ominous: 'After John was arrested (literally, delivered up).' The fate of the Baptist was to be delivered up to his enemies (6: 17-29) 'according to the definite plan and foreknowledge of God' (Acts 2:23) – following a mysterious divine purpose. There is already a hint of the fate of Jesus; the long shadow of the cross has reached to the start of the gospel. Yet now began the preaching of 'the good news of peace', and Mark's sentence, 'the kingdom (reign) of God has come near; repent and believe in the good news' is an apt summing-up of the preaching and message of Jesus. Like the Baptist (Mk 1:4), Jesus called for thorough-going conversion. More urgently, he called on people to embrace the good news. The evangelist intended the words 'believe in the good news' to be taken in the Christian sense of faith in the good news of salvation through Jesus Christ.

Jesus began his mission by summoning disciples. The passage 1:16-20, with two parallel episodes, was shaped by Mark to bring out the nature of Jesus' call and the nature of Christian response; in short, to show what 'following Jesus' means. We are shown that the sovereign call of Jesus evokes the response of those called, a free response as we will learn in the episode of the man who could not bring himself to follow – the man 'who had great possessions' (10: 17-22). These fishermen leave all, nets, boat and father, to follow Jesus without hesitation. The decisive factor is the person of Jesus himself. The episode is stylised, of course. Mark is not intent on describing a scene from the ministry of Jesus. Rather, he is concerned with the theological dimension of a typical call to discipleship. Behind his text, however, is the memory that Jesus called – the initiative was his – and that his immediate disciples, men and women (see 15:40-41), had indeed left all to accompany him on his itinerant mission. We must keep in mind that others had responded to Jesus without taking to the road with him – people like the sisters Martha and Mary of Bethany. There are different ways of true discipleship.

Healer and Exorcist

All four gospels agree that Jesus worked miracles – not just a few but many. In the modern world, many find it difficult to accommodate the notion of miracle; many reject the possibility of miracle. In contrast, in the Graeco-Roman world of Jesus' day, miracles were readily acknowledged. If Jesus did perform miracles, they would be accepted as such by his contemporaries. The majority of his miracles were healings of various diseases. His healing activity was motivated not only by his concern for suffering, his sympathy with the afflicted. It was also a sign of the inbreak of the kingdom. The saving power of God was making its way into the lives of men and women.

Prominent among Jesus' miraculous deeds – especially so in Mark – were exorcisms. This aspect of Jesus' activity can and does upset our modern sensibility. The situation is aggravated by theatrical exploitation of the subject by quite harmful interventions of would-be 'exorcists'. In the world of Jesus, on the other hand, exorcism was readily accepted both in paganism and in Judaism. It is, then, to be expected rather than come as a surprise, that Jesus figured as an exorcist. John P. Meier comments:

> However disconcerting it may be to modern sensibilities, it is fairly certain that Jesus was, among other things, a first-century Jewish exorcist and probably won not a little of his fame and following by practising exorcisms ... Perhaps in no other aspect of

Jesus' ministry does his distance from modern Western culture and scientific technology loom so large and the facile program of making the historical Jesus instantly relevant to present-day men and women seem so ill-conceived. One can approach his exorcisms with greater sympathy if one remembers that Jesus no doubt saw them as part of his overall ministry of healing and liberating the people of Israel from the illnesses and other physical and spiritual evils that beset them. Granted the primitive state of medical knowledge in the first-century Mediterranean world, mental illness, psychosomatic diseases, and such afflictions as epilepsy were often attributed to demonic possession. If Jesus saw himself called to battle against these evils, which diminished the lives of his fellow Israelites, it was quite natural for him, as a first-century Jew, to understand this specific dimension of his ministry in terms of exorcism. All of this simply underscores the obvious: Jesus was a man and a Jew of his times (*A Marginal Jew, Vol 2: Mentor, Message, and Miracles*, New York: Doubleday, 1994, 406-407).

An obvious corollary is that a twenty-first century Jesus would view the situation very differently; he would not be an exorcist. We must adjust our perspective to a first-century worldview.

Exorcism and Healing 1: 22-31
Two distinct episodes are set in the Capernaum synagogue (1:22-28): a teaching of Jesus which provoked the admiration of his hearers and the expulsion of an unclean spirit which awoke reverential fear in the witnesses. Jesus is powerful in word and deed. An intriguing feature of Mark's portrayal of Jesus is that, though he stresses again and again the teaching authority of Jesus, he offers, in comparison with Matthew and Luke, very little of Jesus' teaching. Recognition of Jesus as God's agent is common among 'demons' (see 3:11). This demon acknowledged, besides, that Jesus' mission was designed to destroy the demonic power-structure. Ironically, it is an 'unclean spirit' that draws attention to who Jesus is and the ultimate purpose of his coming: the whole overcoming of evil. No human, before the cross (see 15:39) recognised that Jesus was Son of God. 'Demons' were believed to have preternatural knowledge. We, twenty-first century Christians, have a worldview very different from that of our brother Mark – different from that of our brother

Jesus of Nazareth. We join Mark in acknowledging, in our manner, that Jesus is Lord.

The early Christian community regarded the miracles of Jesus in a twofold light: as a manifestation of the power of God active in Jesus and as signs of the redemption which Jesus wrought. In the healing story of Peter's mother-in-law (1:29-31) the phrase 'he lifted her up' (*egeiró*, 'to lift up' also means 'to raise from the dead') has symbolic meaning. The woman 'lifted' from 'fever' symbolised one formerly prostrate beneath the thrall of sin and now raised up by the Lord and called upon to serve him. Another factor, Jesus leaves himself open to criticism. In his Jewish culture no self-respecting religious leader would take a woman by the hand nor permit himself to be served by this woman.

Summary 1:32-34

We have been shown a typical exorcism and a typical healing. Now, at the close of this specimen day (1:21-34), 'all' the sick and possessed of the town are brought to Jesus (1:32-34). This summarising passage moves the story along. Here, for the first time, appears Mark's so-called 'messianic secret' (v 34). It was firmly Mark's view that no human being could acknowledge in faith and truth that Jesus is Son of God before the paradoxical revelation of his identity through his death on the cross. The element of secrecy concerns not Jesus' messiahship but his identity as Son of God. The divine voice, at baptism and transfiguration, did proclaim Jesus' Sonship. The unclean spirits become guides to the reader! Their being bound to silence is a reminder that, to know and proclaim the truth about Jesus, one must, like the centurion, come to terms with the cross (15: 39).

I Was Sent for this Purpose 1: 35-39

Reference to the prayer of Jesus may give us a proper understanding of the episode. Mark mentions Jesus' prayer on two further occasions: after the multiplication of loaves (6:46) and in Gethsemane (14:35, 39). Each time the true nature of his messiahship is in question and he has to contend with the incomprehension of his disciples (6:52; 14:40). So too, here, the disciples had 'hunted for him'. This is not the attitude of true disciples; this is not the following of Jesus to which they had been called. 'That is what I came out to do': Jesus explains to his disciples that he must not linger to satisfy the curiosity of the people of Capernaum. Luke had correctly caught the Marcan nuance when he wrote: 'for I was sent for this purpose' (Lk 4:43). A closing statement (Mk 1:39) shows the carrying out of the programme sketched in v 38. Again there is a firm reference to Galilee as the privileged place of the mission of Jesus.

You Can Make Me Clean 1:40-45
Leprosy (a term which in the Bible covers a variety of skin diseases [see Leviticus 13]) was regarded as the ultimate uncleanness, which cut the afflicted one off from the community as being a source of ritual defilement for others. The Law was helpless in regard to leprosy; it could only protect the community against the leper. But what the law could not achieve, Jesus accomplished. According to the more widely attested reading (in the Greek manuscripts), Jesus was moved with 'pity' at the petition of the wretched man (v 41). There can be little doubt that 'moved with anger', not nearly so well attested, is the original reading. It is easy to understand why copyists would have changed this into 'moved with pity'; it is incredible that they should have done the reverse. This anger of Jesus was twofold. It was his reaction to a disease which brought him face to face with the ravages of evil – all disease, it was thought, was caused by evil forces. More deeply it was because the unfortunate man had been branded a pariah. His disease had cut him off from social and religious life. If one were to touch him – even his garment – one was rendered 'unclean', unworthy to approach God. Thus can religion distort the graciousness of God.

Jesus' anger at the situation was a facet of his impatience with a religious attitude that puts observance before people. He stepped forward, reached out and firmly laid his hand on the man – no concern with uncleanness there! The man was healed. The law (Lev 14:2-32) specified that one who claimed to be healed of leprosy should have the cure verified by a priest. In bidding the man to carry out the prescription, Jesus intended something more. 'As a testimony to them' (v 44) is to be taken as a challenge to the priesthood and their view of things – it is a testimony *against* them (see 6:11). Jesus was already aware that the priests did not look kindly upon his mission. Who are the 'lepers', the outcasts, of our day? One readily thinks of, among others, those who suffer from AIDS. Does one need to ask how Jesus would treat them? He would surely be 'moved with anger' at how unkindly they are categorised by some 'Christians'.

Conflict 2:1–3:6

2 ¹When he returned to Capernaum after some days, it was reported that he was at home. ²So many gathered around that there was no longer room for them, not even in front of the door; and he was speaking the word to them. ³Then some people came, bringing to him a paralysed man, carried by four of them. ⁴And when they could not bring him to Jesus because of the crowd, they removed the roof above him; and after having dug through it, they let down the mat on which the paralytic lay. ⁵When Jesus saw their faith, he said to the paralytic, 'Son, your sins are forgiven.' ⁶Now some of the scribes were sitting there, **questioning in their hearts**, ⁷'Why does this fellow speak in this way? It is blasphemy! Who can forgive sins but God alone?' ⁸At once Jesus perceived in his spirit that they were discussing these questions among themselves and he said to them, 'Why do you **raise such questions in your hearts**? ⁹Which is easier, to say to the paralytic, "Your sins are forgiven" or to say, "Stand up and **take your mat** and walk?" ¹⁰But so that you may know that the Son of Man has authority on earth to forgive sins' – he said to the paralytic – ¹¹'I say to you, stand up, **take your mat** and go to your home.' ¹²And he stood up, and immediately took the mat and went out before all of them; so that they were all amazed and glorified God, saying, 'We have never seen anything like this!'

¹³Jesus went out again beside the sea; the whole crowd gathered around him, and he taught them. ¹⁴As he was walking along, he saw Levi son of Alphaeus sitting at the tax booth, and he said to him, 'Follow me.' And he got up and followed him.

¹⁵And as he sat at dinner in Levi's house, many tax collectors and sinners were also sitting with Jesus and his disciples – for there were many who followed him. ¹⁶When the scribes of the Pharisees saw that he was eating with sinners and tax collectors, they said to his disciples, 'Why does he eat with tax collectors and sinners?' ¹⁷When Jesus heard this, he said to them, 'Those who are well have no need of a physician, but those who are sick; I have come not to call the righteous but sinners.'

¹⁸Now John's disciples and the Pharisees were fasting and people came and said to him, 'Why do John's disciples and the disciples of the Pharisees fast, but your disciples do not fast?' ¹⁹Jesus said to them, 'The wedding guests cannot fast while the bridegroom is with them, can they? As long as they have the bridegroom with them, they cannot fast. ²⁰The days will come when the bridegroom is taken away from them, and they will fast on that day. ²¹No one sews a piece of unshrunk cloth on an old cloak; otherwise, the patch pulls away from it, the new from the old, and a worse tear is made. ²²And no one puts new wine into old wineskins; otherwise, the wine will burst the skins, and the wine is lost, and so are the skins;

but one puts new wine into fresh wineskins.'

²³One Sabbath he was going through the grainfields; and as they made their way the disciples began to pluck heads of grain. ²⁴The Pharisees said to him, 'Look, why are they doing what is not lawful on the Sabbath?' ²⁵And he said to them, 'Have you never read what David did when he and his companions were hungry and in need of food? ²⁶He entered the house of God when Abiathar was high priest, and ate the bread of the Presence, which it is not lawful for any but the priests to eat, and he gave some to his companions.' ²⁷Then he said to them, 'The sabbath was made for humankind, and not humankind for the Sabbath; ²⁸so the Son of Man is lord even of the sabbath.'

3 ¹Again he entered the synagogue, and a man was there who had a withered hand. ²They watched him to see whether he would cure him on the sabbath, so that they might accuse him. ³And he said to the man who had the withered hand, 'Come forward.' ⁴Then he said to them, 'Is it lawful to do good or to do harm on the Sabbath, to save life or to kill?' But they were silent. ⁵He looked around at them with anger; he was grieved at their hardness of heart and said to the man, 'Stretch out your hand.' He stretched it out, and his hand was restored. ⁶The Pharisees went out and immediately conspired with the Herodians against him, how to destroy him.

Jesus had been carrying out his mission in Galilee, teaching, healing, exorcising. Soon comes confrontation – with various opponents. It is documented in a series of five controversies: on forgiveness of sins (2:1-12), on eating with tax collectors and sinners (2:13-17), on fasting (2:18-22), on grainfields on the sabbath 92:23-28), and concerning healing on the sabbath (3:1-6). These conflicts are arranged in progressive order. At the cure of the paralytic the opposition to Jesus was latent: the scribes 'questioned in their hearts' (2:6-7). During the meal in the house of Levi they addressed the disciples, aiming through them at Jesus (2:16) while with regard to fasting they questioned Jesus about an omission of his disciples (2:18). In the matter of the grainfields, the charge against the disciples is a direct violation of the law (2:24). In the final episode the adversaries spy on Jesus (3:2) and then meet together to plot his destruction.

Mark has arranged the five episodes in a chiastic pattern:

A. 2:1-9 – cure by Jesus – silence of the adversaries – 'questioning in
   their hearts;'
  B. 2:10-12 – declaration on the Son of Man;
    C. 2:13-17 – action of Jesus – reaction of opponents;
      D. 2:18-22 – sayings on Bridegroom and Newness;
    C' 2:23-26 – action of disciples – reaction of opponents;
  B' 2:27-28 – declaration on the Son of Man
A' 3: 1-6 – cure by Jesus – silence of the adversaries – 'hardness of
   heart.'

The plan clearly shows the articulation of the ensemble ABC and
C'B'A' around the point D. We must take account of the thematic
unity of the two groupings and respect the role of the central text 2:
18-22.

One purpose of the composition of this section was to illustrate and
explain the opposition to Jesus, the hostility that led to his death.
We are shown that the opposition came not from the people but
from the religious authorities who were determined to preserve the
established religious order. Because they were unable to understand him they ended by determining to destroy him. And this situation in the mission of Jesus has a bearing too on the hostile attitude
of official Judaism to Mark's community (see 13:9)

At the same time, the section sets the teaching of Jesus in relief: the
section is not only apologetic but is markedly catechetical as well.
The fact is that each of the separate units which make up the complex is not only a conflict story, a debate with adversaries, but a pronouncement story, leading to a declaration or pronouncement of
Jesus. We can see that the saving message of each is to be found in a
saying of the Lord – the stories are so many illustrations of that
'new teaching with authority behind it' (1:27). If we set out the five
climactic sayings one after another we can readily perceive how
valuable they are for an understanding of the Christian gospel:
    The Son of Man has authority on earth to forgive sins (2:10).
    I have come not to call the righteous but sinners (2:17).
    Can the wedding guests fast while the Bridegroom is with
    them? (2:19).
    The Son of Man is lord even of the sabbath (2:28).
    Is it lawful to do good or to do harm on the sabbath, to save life
    or to kill? (3: 4).

These sayings – all of them in part or in whole Christian formul-ations – have a vital bearing on the content of the gospel message and on the early church's understanding of its Lord.

The Paralytic and Forgiveness 2:1-12

Several indications point to the composite character of this passage. On the whole it seems reasonable to regard vv 1-5a, 11-12 as a coherent miracle story, corresponding to the classic scheme of the healing of a paralytic, as in John 5: 5-9; Acts 9: 32-35. Here, however, the story is augmented by a passage on the remission of sins (vv 5b-10). Mark has converted a miracle story into a controversy story. The evangelist is telling us that the cure of the paralytic was intended to manifest the sin-forgiving power of the Son of Man. In the early kerygma, remission of sin was regarded as intrinsic to the experi-ence of being Christian. Thus Acts 10:43 states, 'All the prophets testify about him [Jesus] that everyone who believes in him receives forgiveness of sins through his name.' A divine prerogative has been granted to Jesus. In the light of this and similar texts it is evid-ent that early Christians proclaimed the forgiveness of sins as a pre-sent fact.

The emergence of the forgiveness of sins debate in the gospel is an indication that it was a live issue in Mark's community. Their asser-tion of forgiveness of sins on earth, an assertion made in the name of Jesus, was blasphemy to their Jewish adversaries – 'Who can for-give sins but God alone?' (2:7). Their defence was in their claim of a share in the authority of the eschatological Son of Man (v 10). For Mark the full revelation of the Son of Man was in his suffering, death, and resurrection and so was accessible only to believers. When, however, those who believe in Jesus seek to live and act in the Spirit of Jesus, they participated in his power to forgive sins. The story of 2:1-12 became a vindication of the church's claim to declare forgiveness of sins in the name of Jesus (see Jn 20:23), a for-giveness achieved in baptism.

Table Fellowship with Outcasts 2:13-17

The call of Levi (2:14), parallel to the call of the first disciples (1:16-20), serves as an introduction to the pronouncement story 2:15-17. The whole passage (2:13-17) illustrated Jesus' attitude towards out-casts and strikingly brought to the fore the amply attested fact that

Jesus' concern for outcasts was a scandal to the religious authorities. We know that table fellowship (between Christians of Jewish and Gentile backgrounds) was something of a problem in the early church (see Acts 11:3; Gal 2:12); it would have been crucial in the matter of eucharistic table fellowship. It may well be that this interest accounts for the formation and preservation of the original story.

For the evangelist, however, the episode was closely associated with the preceding cure of the paralytic (2:1-12). There the centre of interest was the authority of the Son of Man to forgive sins; here it is the presence of the 'physician' able to 'cure' the 'sick', that is, sinners. The fact that Jesus associated with sinners was a sign not only of the remission of sins but of the presence of one who could remit sins. In the Old Testament, Yahweh alone is the Physician, the healer (see Hosea 14:4; Jer 3:22; 17:4; 30:17; Sirach 38:1-15), and healing is a sign of the messianic age (see Is 61:1; Mt 10:1, 8). Against this background, Jesus' reference to himself as 'physician' – 'Those who are well have no need of a physician, but those who are sick; I have come not to call the righteous but sinners' – implied more than a proverbial justification of his conduct. If he ate with sinners it was because the sick had need of the physician. For those who could see, his calculated practice of breaking bread with sinners was a declaration that the kingdom had indeed 'come near' (1:15); the physician was at work. 'The righteous' believe that they already know what right relationship with God entails. They have no need of this physician!

On Fasting and Newness 2:18-22
This passage contains a pronouncement story (vv 18-20) to which two sayings, on patches and wineskins, have been added (vv 21-22). The main story manifests, yet again, the presence of the kingdom: the fact that the disciples of Jesus did not fast brought home to those who could understand that the Bridegroom was with them. This was, already, a Christian claim. While the image of wedding feast expressed the joy of the messianic age, neither in the Old Testament nor in early Judaism was the Messiah presented as bridegroom. On the other hand, Yahweh was cast as spouse of his covenant people (see Hosea 2:19; Is 54:3-6; 62:5; Jer 2:2). Jesus' implied claim to be bridegroom is a claim on a par with that of authority to forgive sins.

If Jesus was bridegroom, then he had ushered in the joyful time of salvation. His disciples were guests at a wedding feast; it was surely not the time or place for fasting. Indeed, during the ministry, 'they cannot fast'! (v 19). Jesus was equivalently claiming that, in his ministry, the kingdom was already present. And there is a further factor. It is important that Jesus is replying to a question put to him by outsiders – 'people' (v 18). His reply not only explained why, unlike groups such as the Baptist's followers and the Pharisees, his disciples did not fast; it asserted the distinctiveness of his group.

> What is unheard of is for some individual Jewish teacher to tell outsiders that what marks off his disciples from every other pious Jewish group is that in principle his disciples cannot fast at all because of his particular message and ministry. In effect, then, at least on this one issue of voluntary fasting, Jesus distinguished his disciples from all other Jews. (J. P. Meier, *A Marginal Jew*, Vol 2, 450).

Jesus was thereby making a remarkable claim for his own person and mission.

But Mark has a problem. Despite the known praxis of Jesus, it is evident that fasting became a practice among Christians. He has to produce a relevant codicil (v 20) to the declaration of Jesus. The bridegroom was manifestly Jesus and his being 'taken away' was a veiled reference to his impending death. It is an echo of Is 53:8 – 'By a perversion of justice he was taken away.' The eschatological prophecy ('the days will come') of Mk 2:20, put in the mouth of Jesus, announced, in place of the present wedding atmosphere, a time of bereavement: Jesus will no longer be physically present. If, now they cannot fast, then they will fast. A practice of fasting, current in Mark's day, has been duly justified.

Through Grainfields on the Sabbath 2:23-28

Though it appears as a sabbath controversy, the passage does not directly regard the problem of sabbath observance. The focus is on the significance of an incident in David's flight from Saul (1 Samuel 21: 1-6). He and his men had come to the sanctuary of Nob where the priest Ahimelech (Mark, mistakenly, names Abiathar, son of Ahimelech) aware of their need, gave them the consecrated loaves, reserved for the priests: in case of need, law yields to human concern. In Mark the essential factor remains the comparison between David and Jesus. The interest is christological: Jesus, as God's anointed son, has the same freedom as David in respect of the law. Mark developed his christological thrust in v 28 (see 2:10) in the light of 2:23-27: 'So the Son of Man is lord even of the sabbath.' The matter was of importance because sabbath observance was a lively issue in the early church (see Lk 14:10-17; Jn 5:1-19; 9:1-11). At an early stage Christians began to observe not the Jewish sabbath but the day of resurrection, 'the Lord's day' (Rev 1:10); this, of course, brought them into conflict with Judaism. They maintained that their Lord had set the sabbath free and their distinctive observance was traced back to his authority. The Marcan Jesus had claimed God-given authority to define the true meaning of the sabbath: 'The sabbath was made for humankind, and not humankind for the sabbath' (v 27). Decoded, this reads: religion is to serve men and women; men and women are not to be enslaved by religion. He had defined the true meaning of religion – it is *for* men and women

To Save life or to Kill 3: 1-6

The fifth conflict story is the climax of the series. Here Jesus himself is more aggressive and the plot against him (v 6) points to the inevitable end of the persistent hostility. But the issue was, too, of immediate interest to Mark's community. If Christians had chosen to observe the Lord's day (Sunday) rather than the Jewish sabbath, they had, nonetheless, opted for a form of sabbath observance. The question was: How far to push that observance and in what spirit? The challenge of Jesus and his deed of mercy (v 4) will have given them their principle and their pattern.

A trap had been set for Jesus: a man with a withered hand was positioned prominently in the synagogue. Jesus was angry. They were callously using this poor man as bait. One does not treat people so. They were making a mockery of the sabbath. He healed the man; the Pharisees promptly accused Jesus of an infringement of sabbath observance. He viewed the matter in a wholly different light and challenged their attitude. In forbidding healing on the sabbath the rabbis would equivalently admit that, on this day, moral values were reversed: it was forbidden to 'do good' and prescribed to 'do evil'! (Note the querulous synagogue leader of Luke 13:14 in reaction to Jesus' healing of a crippled woman on the sabbath: 'There

are six days in which work ought to be done; come on those days to
be cured, and not on the sabbath day.'). The real issue is no longer
what one is permitted to do; it is the obligation of doing good at all
times and in all circumstances. Jesus asked: 'Is it lawful to do good
or to do harm on the Sabbath, to save life or to kill?' How sad that
the spirit of legalism has so regularly and so firmly asserted itself in
the Christian church. We have been so eager to multiply rules and
to impose them, so anxious to measure our Christianity by the
punctiliousness of our 'observance'.

B. He Came to His Own 3:7–6:6a

Crowds by the Lakeside 3:7-12

⁷Jesus departed with his disciples to the sea, and **a great multitude** from Galilee followed him, ⁸hearing all that he was doing. They came to him, **a great multitude**, from Judea, Jerusalem, Idumea, beyond the Jordan, and the regions around Tyre and Sidon. ⁹He told his disciples to have a boat ready for him because of the crowd, so that they would not crush him; ¹⁰for he had cured many, so that all who had diseases pressed upon him to touch him. ¹¹Whenever the unclean spirits saw him, they fell down before him and shouted, 'You are the Son of God!' ¹²But he sternly ordered them not to make him known.

Together with the call of the Twelve (3:13-19a) this summary shows like a ray of light breaking between dark clouds of hostility (2:1–3:6 and 3:19b-35). Coming after the conflict stories, which underlined the prejudice of the scribes and Pharisees and their rejection of Jesus, the passage points again to the enthusiasm of the people and to the perception of the evil spirits who discerned what the religious authorities failed to see. A great multitude came to Jesus not only from friendly Galilee but from much further afield. Mark is at pains to stress not only that the Jewish people crowded to Jesus from every quarter of the land but that Jesus was evoking a response of faith among Gentiles. The theological rather than geographical interest of the evangelist is indicated in the bracket phrase 'a great multitude' (vv 7, 8).

The Twelve 3:13-19a

¹³He went up the mountain and called to him those whom he wanted, and they came to him, ¹⁴and **he appointed twelve**, whom he also named apostles, to be with him and to be sent out to proclaim the message, ¹⁵and to have authority to cast out demons. ¹⁶So **he appointed the twelve:** Simon (to whom he gave the name Peter); ¹⁷James son of Zebedee and John the brother of James (to whom he gave the name *Boanerges*, that is, Sons of Thunder); ¹⁸and Andrew, and Philip, and Bartholomew, and Matthew, and Thomas, and

James son of Alphaeus, and Thaddaeus, and Simon the Cananaean, ¹⁹and Judas Iscariot, who **betrayed him**.

The bracket-phrase, 'he appointed twelve' underlines the immediate role of this inner group. In the first place they are 'to be with him'; they are to have close personal relationship with Jesus – forming a new family, in short. And from now on the Twelve do remain constantly with him (until they fail him, spectacularly, 14:50). In the second place, the Twelve were commissioned to be sent out, to preach, and to have authority over demons. While the evangelist had the sending out of 6:7-13 in mind, his vocabulary shows that he looked beyond it. The Greek words *apostellein*, 'to send out', and *keryssein*, 'to preach', are terms which the apostolic church used to describe its mission. Mark was conscious of the post-resurrection missionary situation. The Twelve were to preach and to do; the word of God is proclaimed in word and action together.

His Own Received Him Not 3:19b-35

^{19b}Then he went home; ²⁰and the crowd came together again, so that they could not even eat. ²¹When his family heard it, they went out to restrain him, for people were saying, 'he has gone out of his mind.'

²²And the scribes who came down from Jerusalem said, 'he has Beelzebul, and by the ruler of the demons he casts out demons.' ²³And he called them to him, and spoke to them in parables. 'How can Satan cast out Satan? ²⁴If a kingdom is divided against itself, that kingdom cannot stand. ²⁵And if a house is divided against itself, that house will not be able to stand. ²⁶And if Satan has risen up against himself and is divided, he cannot stand, but his end has come. ²⁷But no one can enter a strong man's house and plunder his property without first tying up the strong man; then indeed the house can be plundered. ²⁸Truly I tell you, people will be forgiven for their sins and whatever blasphemies they utter; ²⁹but whoever blasphemes against the Holy Spirit can never have forgiveness, but is guilty of an eternal sin' – ³⁰for they had said, 'He has an unclean spirit.'

³¹Then his mother and his brothers came; and standing outside, they sent to him and called him. ³²A crowd was sitting around him; and they said to him, 'Your mother and your brothers and sisters are outside, asking for you,' ³³and he replied, 'Who are my mother and my brothers?' ³⁴And looking at those who sat around him, he said, 'Here are my mother and my brothers! ³⁵Whoever does the will of God is my brother and sister and mother.'

Mark's distinctive 'sandwich' technique points us, unerringly,

towards an understanding of the passage 3:19b-35 – the episode of
the scribes is sandwiched between the two sections on the family of
Jesus (3:29b-21, [22-30], 31-35). It is his pointer that 'slices' and 'filling' be taken as a unit. In v 21 the Nazareth family, concerned for
Jesus, had come to 'restrain' him. They wanted to put him away for
his own good: 'He has gone out of his mind.' Then emerged 'the
scribes who came down from Jerusalem': official Jewish reaction;
Jesus was under investigation. Verse 20 contains two accusations:
he was possessed by Beelzebul, an evil spirit; his exorcisms were
wrought 'by the ruler of the demons', that is, Satan. These scribes
had witnessed Jesus' healings; they had passed judgement. Like
Job's comforters, they were complacently sure of the truth of their
theology. Jesus was one who did not observe the Sabbath, one who
freely associated with sinners. His conduct was an affront to the
holy God. Jesus' power – they could not deny the healings – was
surely not from God. That left one other source! He was casting out
the malign influences that caused sickness through the power of
Satan – evil itself!

The accusations are taken up in turn in vv 28-29 and 27 – this
reverse order treatment is normal. The charge that Jesus cast out
demons by the power of Satan was answered by denial that Satan
was divided against himself. Can a divided kingdom stand firm?
Can a dynasty, riven within, survive? And if Satan was suffering
setbacks (the healings and exorcisms) might it not be that a power
stronger than Satan was about? The explanatory editorial comment
in v 30 – 'for they said, "he has an unclean spiri"' – shows that the
charge of blasphemy against the Holy Spirit (vv 28-29) is to be taken
as Jesus' response to the accusation of being possessed. That comment makes clear that 'blasphemy against the Holy Spirit' means
the attribution of the exorcisms of Jesus (and, by implication) his
whole mission, wrought by the power of the Spirit, to a malign
source. The 'sin' or 'blasphemy' is not so much an offence against
the Spirit as humankind's refusal of the salvation which God was
offering through the Spirit active in Jesus. The whole presence and
ministry of Jesus made abundantly clear that, from God's side,
there is no such thing as an unforgivable sin: 'Truly I tell you, people will be forgiven ['divine passive': God will forgive] for their sins
and whatever blasphemies they utter.' The story obviously took for

granted Jesus' reputation as an exorcist. Not the exorcisms, but the source of them, was questioned.

The New Family of Jesus 3:31-35

The family was still about (3:31-32). Seated in the crowded house, Jesus was told that his mother and brothers were outside, wanting to speak with him – wanting to restrain him! (v 21). Too much had happened too quickly; Jesus was lost to them, and they sensed it. Jesus looked at those inside who crowded around, hanging on his words. He had lost his natural family; but he had gained another family. His mother and brother and sisters were not outside – they were right there before him. Those who hear and do the will of the Abba are, now and always, Jesus' brother and sister and mother – the faithful women and men of God (vv 33-35).

He Spoke In Parables 4:1-34

[1]Again he began to teach beside the sea. Such a very large crowd gathered around him that he got into a boat on the sea and sat there, while the whole crowd was beside the sea on the land. [2]He began to teach them many things in parables, and in his teaching he said to them: [3]'Listen! A sower went out to sow. [4]And as he sowed, some seed fell on the path, and the birds came and ate it up. [5]Other seed fell on rocky ground, where it did not have much soil, and it sprang up quickly, since it had no depth of soil. [6]And when the sun rose, it was scorched; and since it had no root, it withered away. [7]Other seed fell among thorns, and the thorns grew up and choked it and it yielded no grain. [8]Other seed fell into good soil and brought forth grain, growing up and increasing and yielding thirty and sixty and a hundredfold.'[9]And he said, 'Let anyone with ears to hear listen!'
[10]When he was alone, those who were around him with the twelve asked him about the parables. [11]And he said to them, 'To you has been given the secret of the kingdom of God, but for those outside, everything comes in parables: [12]in order that

> they may indeed look, but not perceive,
> and may indeed listen, but not understand;
> so that they may not turn again and be forgiven.'

[13]And he said to them, 'Do you not understand this parable? Then how will you understand all the parables? [14]The sower sows the word. [15]These are the ones on the path where the word is sown; when they hear, Satan immediately comes and takes away the word that is sown in them. [16]And these are the ones sown on rocky ground; when they hear the word, they immediately receive it with joy. [17]But they have no root, and endure only for a while; then, when trouble or persecution arises on account of the word, immedi-

ately they fall away. [18]And others are those sown among the thorns; these are ones who hear the word, [19]but the cares of the world, and the lure of wealth, and the desire for other things come in and choke the word, and it yields nothing. [20]And these are the ones sown on the good soil; they hear the word and accept it and bear fruit, thirty and sixty and a hundredfold.'

[21]He said to them, 'Is a lamp brought in to be put under the bushel basket, or under the bed, and not on the lampstand? [22]For there is nothing hidden, except to be disclosed; nor is anything secret, except to come to light. [23]Let anyone with ears to hear listen!' [24]And he said to them, 'Pay attention to what you hear; the measure you give will be the measure you get, and still more will be given you. [25]For to those who have, more will be given; and from those who have nothing, even what they have will be taken away.'

[26]He also said, 'The kingdom of God is as if someone would scatter seed on the ground, [27]and would sleep and rise night and day, and the seed would sprout and grow, he does not know how. [28]The earth produces of itself, first the stalk, then the heads, then the full grain in the head. [29]But when the grain is ripe, at once he goes in with the sickle, because the harvest has come.'

[30]He also said, 'With what can we compare the kingdom of God, or what parable will we use for it? [31]It is like as mustard seed, which, when sown upon the ground, is the smallest of all the seeds on earth; [32]yet when it is sown it grows up and becomes the greatest of all shrubs, and puts forth large branches, so that the birds of the air can make nests in its shade.'

[33]With many such parables he spoke the word to them, as they were able to hear it; [34]he did not speak to them except in parables, but he explained everything in private to his disciples

Parables

Jesus taught, strikingly, in parables. We associate parable so closely with him indeed that it might seem as though he had created the parable. Rather, he made brilliant use of a genre which was already of long tradition. The Greek word *parabolé* means a juxtaposition or comparison of two realities. In classical rhetoric, the strict parable had only one point of reference and might be described as an extended simile. According to Aristotle, parables are of two kinds: true events taken from history, and the imaginatively fictional; his preference was for the first sort. In the Old Testament, however, while the context is history, the imaginative parable abounds. Jesus, and the New Testament writers, followed the Bible, not Aristotle. The Old Testament, then, is the proper background of gospel parable study.

Mashal

The Septuagint translators (the Septuagint is the pre-Christian Greek version of the Hebrew Scripture) had lit on *parabolé* as their preferred rendering of the Hebrew *mashal*. That can be: a representation or a type, a simile or a metaphor, a maxim or a pithy saying, a symbol or a riddle. It might carry, also, the aura of a 'dark saying,' implying mystery. The bewildering range of meaning may be gauged from the fact that each proverb in the Book of Proverbs – two-line couplets in the main – is a *mashal* (e.g. Prov 10:1), while each of the elaborate speeches of Job is also termed *mashal* (e.g. Job 29-31). In the gospels the term *parabolé* includes not only parables but aphorism – a pithy, arresting saying, complete in itself, e.g. 'The Sabbath was made for humankind, and not humankind for the Sabbath' (Mk 2:27). Both parable and aphorism invite reflection and can be more challenging and effective than straightforward statements.

By Jesus' day the parable had become a familiar form in rabbinical preaching. It had a history, as witness Nathan's clever parable in 2 Samuel 12:1-4 – with a hapless David toppling into the parabolic trap (12:5-7). In general, biblical parable drew material from daily life and followed set meanings: vineyard, sons, servants represented Israel, king or father meant God, feast indicated the messianic age, harvest, the judgement. When Jesus chose to speak in parables he was following a convention familiar to his hearers.

It has long been scholarly practice to take the gospel parables out of their context in order to deal with them as a genre on their own. But, surely, it is right to insist that parables ought to be studied in their one sure *Sitz im Leben* – the place of a parable in a particular gospel. A gospel parable can be rightly understood in its gospel context. It is not possible confidently to situate any parable in the historical ministry of Jesus. One cannot really get back there. But each parable does appear at a particular place in each gospel. We can recognise its literary setting and ask what it is doing just there. One is not thereby suggesting that the gospel setting of a parable exhausts the potential of its challenge.

Parables in Mark

In chapter 4 of Mark (precisely, Mk 4:1-34) we have a collection of parables and, in vv 10-12, the evangelist's theory of the purpose of parables:

[10]When he was alone, those who were around him with the twelve asked him about the parables. [11]And he said to them, 'To you has been given the secret of the kingdom of God, but for those outside, everything comes in parables, [12]in order that

> they may indeed look, but not perceive,
> and may indeed listen, but not understand;
> so that they may not turn again and be forgiven.'

No treatment of gospel parables can avoid trying to come to terms with the implication of Mk 4:10-12. On the face of it, one is told that Jesus spoke in parables in order that his hearers should not understand. That such might have been his purpose is so alien to the character of Jesus as to be incredible. We must look to the evangelist for an explanation. It is already instructive that Matthew (13:10-17) has notably tailored Mark's text to his purpose. He has distinguished between a time when Jesus had spoken openly to 'the Jews' and a time when, in reaction to their rejection of him, he reverted to parabolic teaching. Each in his manner, Matthew and Mark were facing up to a problem which exercised the early church: the obduracy of Israel (see Rom 9-11).

Mark, for his part, seems to have taken a staunchly deterministic approach: there are those who, divinely enlightened, understand and accept the message of the parables, while 'those outside' fatally misunderstand and reject. In Mark's parable theory passage the Isaian text (Is 6:9-10) is perfectly in place: unreceptivity is presented as something foreseen, even ordained, by God. Besides, there is the esoteric facet of a parable. In Mark, while parables are spoken in public (see 4:3-34), their meaning is (in theory) grasped only within the inner circle of disciples. This is particularly suited to Mark's gospel with its emphasis on the mysterious nature of Jesus.

In its Isaian setting the declaration of Is 6:9-10 is a forceful and paradoxical way of proclaiming what is inevitably going to happen: the prophet's preaching will not be heeded. In the Marcan text the evangelist is addressing the obduracy of Israel. Why did, by and large, the Jewish contemporaries of Jesus not hearken to his message, not come to understand him? And why did the Jewish people continue to resist the preaching of Mark's community? Mark's answer is stark: their rejection of the gospel fell within God's plan. Early Christian thinkers tended to account for the rejection of the message of Jesus and of the apostles by asserting that such was the will of God (see Rom 9:18-19; 10:16-21; 11:7-10; Jn 12:37-41; Acts 28:25-28). They were influenced by a currently accepted apocalyptic view of a deterministic will of God (see Dan 12:10; Rev 22:11). Mark's distinctive contribution was to exploit the mysterious aspect of parable in that direction. Ultimately he was, in tortuous fashion, asserting that Israel's inexplicable behaviour had a divine purpose. It was Paul's conviction also, expressed in a similarly tortuous manner (Rom 9-11).

Of course the New Testament writers, like their Old Testament predecessors, maintained that people carry responsibility for their actions, and this responsibility was not taken to be voided by the apocalyptic doctrine of determinism. In accord with this belief in a deterministic will of God, Mark proposed that Jesus had taught in mysterious parables; to the disciples alone was revealed the secret of the kingdom (4:11). Through them his teaching would be preserved and passed on. Yet, Mark will go out of his way to insist that the disciples did not comprehend Jesus and did not grasp his teaching. His statement that God had granted the secret (mystery) of the kingdom to some while hiding it from others relates to the situation of his day and looks beyond the specific problem of official Jewish rejection of Jesus and of the good news. He had in mind the situation illustrated in the explanation of the parable of the Sower (4:14-20). His point was that for all those whose 'hardness of heart,' whose resistance to the good news, placed a barrier to the invitation and challenge of Jesus, the parables were riddles to which they had no key. He was sure that God alone could open hearts to the word and bring it to harvest. All of this is the viewpoint of the Marcan Jesus, that is to say, of the evangelist himself.

Sower and Explanation (4:1-9, 13-20)
The text of the parable of the Sower (4:1-9) is notably Semitic and the lines of it are simple and clear. But because we can no longer determine its setting in the mission of Jesus we cannot be sure of its original meaning. It is commonly taken to be a parable of the kingdom; it is not at all clear that it was ever meant to be such. What is beyond doubt is that, for Mark, it a parable of the word; it is quite likely that this, too, was Jesus' intent. There is notable emphasis on hearing: 'Listen' (v 3), 'Let anyone with ears to hear listen!' (v 9), an

emphasis sustained throughout the parable passage. It surely cannot be claimed that Mark had turned the parable from its original purpose. On the other hand, the parable might be characterised as a parable of the soils; it is where the seed falls and what happens to it that are decisive.

Structurally, the parable of the Sower falls into two parts: the first part (vv 4-7) is negative – the grain and seedlings and young plants perish; the second part (v 8) is positive – the rest of the grain flourishes and the yield is startling. 'Listen' (v 3) echoes the 'Hear' of Deut 6:4. For Mark the admonition highlighted, from the outset, the importance, sustained throughout his narrative, of 'hearing' (see v 9) and also suggested that parables were meant to provoke thought. The farmer sowed haphazardly: on the path, on rocks, among thorns (the incongruous, a feature of several parables) – also, happily, on fertile soil. The story had something more than farming in mind. The parable was about the hearers of the word – the different soils. The parable is allegory, as the explanation (vv 14-20) insists. Its main concern is the word and the hearers of the word. The hearer is exhorted to receive the word in faith and keep it with steadfastness. And the 'word' was not only Jesus' proclamation of the coming kingdom but, more immediately for Mark, the proclamation of the Christian message. Here, too, is the counter to the determinism of vv 11-12, stressing human responsibility and the need for a response to the proclamation. The question of Jesus in v 13 points to another dimension of the parable: it is the key to understanding all other parables. It is so because it is concerned with the presupposition of all parables, the word sown by Jesus. It is, then, a parable not only on the hearing of the word but on the right hearing of parables.

The explanation of the Sower (vv 14-20) is a commentary which takes up and explains each phrase of the parable. Its language shows it to be a product of the early church which reflects the missionary experience of early Christians. Noteworthy is the attention to the various types of soil. But this was already a feature of the parable. The explanation builds on what was already there; it does not give a new and different twist. The seed is the gospel preaching. The word is sown in the hearers; it is 'seeded' in them. Four categories of hearers are distinguished in terms of where the seed had fallen: 'on the path,' 'on rocky ground,' 'among the thorns,' on 'the good soil.' The fate of the word was different in each case. In this allegory the 'seed' is not only the word but, too, the hearers of the word!

The explanation is there because Christians had, perforce, to acknowledge that few had really taken to heart Jesus' word. They asked the question: Why such a gulf between them and those who would not see? They found an answer in this parable. How could they have expected it to be otherwise? Think of what happens when the sower scatters his seed. Not every seed bears fruit. Much is lost for one reason or another. This understanding led them to delineate the forms of resistance to the word. Many people were like those on the path: the word did not reach them as though the devil had swiped it away at the very moment of receiving. Or, many people seemed like shallow growth: they were ready to receive, but were unable to persevere. Or, many people like seed under thorns: they heard, but the word lost its significance because they were choked by cares and distractions. The major concern of the explanation was the structure of human life itself. The shallow mind, the hard heart, worldly preoccupation, persecution – these were precisely the obstacles which frustrated the growth of faith. The explanation presupposed a period when Christian faith was tested by such factors. It offered warning and encouragement. And Mark presented it as a word of Jesus.

Wisdom Sayings 4: 21-25

This is a passage built up of five separate sayings arranged in the pairs vv 21-22 and vv 24-25 with v 23 acting as a connecting link relating them to the parable of the Sower. The formula, 'And he said to them' (vv 21, 24), indicates that they are Marcan inclusions. For Mark the resultant 'parable' clarifies his viewpoint expressed in vv 1-12: just as it is the function of a lamp to give light, so the parables of Jesus are meant to enlighten. The 'hid and secret' of v 22 recall the 'mystery' of v 11; it is conceded that the mystery of the kingdom is hidden for a time – but only for a time. What is now hidden will eventually be revealed to all. The evangelist's meaning is probably that though the mystery of the kingdom was hidden during the mission of Jesus, it was destined to be proclaimed abroad after the resurrection (see 9:9).

The second pair of sayings (vv 24-25) is, in the setting, obscure. 'Pay attention to what you hear' means, carefully consider what you hear, weigh up its meaning. The proverbial saying (v 24b) gives the reason for heeding. This saying occurs in Mt 7:2 and Lk 6:38 in a context of judgement – you will be judged in the measure you judge others – and it is obviously at home in that context. But Mark sets it in relation to the parables and its sense, for him, seems to be: your attention to the teaching will be the measure of the profit you will derive from it. The second saying (v 25) may have been a popular proverb. The other synoptists have the saying also after the parable of the Talents/Pounds (Mt 25:9; Lk 19:26). Here Mark seemingly takes it to mean that the spiritual insight which denotes openness to the teaching of Jesus (v 24) will be deepened by God (the passive 'will be given' implies God as the agent); and, conversely, indifference to the message of the parable will lead to a loss of whatever insight one may have had. It is obvious that none of these sayings originally referred to the parabolic teaching of Jesus. Mark has chosen to connect them with his own parable theory; his insertion of them here makes that much clear at least. For the rest, we cannot be sure of the precise meaning they held for him.

The Growing Seed and the Mustard Seed 4:26-32

The parable of the Seed Growing to Harvest (4:26-29) is proper to Mark. It seems best to take it as a parable of contrast between the inactivity of the sower (after the initial sowing) and the certainty of harvest. The sower goes his way; the seed sprouts and grows without him taking anxious thought. It is God who brings about the growth of the kingdom. Paul had learned the lesson of the parable: 'I planted, Apollos watered, but God gave the growth' (1 Cor 3:6). It may be that, originally, it was Jesus' reply to those who looked, impatiently, for a forceful intervention of God. Or it may have been meant to give assurance to those of the disciples who had become discouraged because little seemed to be happening. Mark surely takes it in the latter sense. Jesus encouraged his disciples: in spite of hindrance and apathy the seed was being sown. Its growth is the work of God who will bring it to harvest.

The parable of the Mustard Seed (4:30-32) is another parable of contrast; but again the idea of growth must be given due weight. Contrast between insignificant beginning and mighty achievement is primary – but the seed does grow into a plant. The detail of branches in which birds nest (v 32) manifestly recalls Ezek 17:23. In Mark's view, the proclamation of the kingdom will bring all nations within its scope (see 13:10). The parable would have been the reply of Jesus to an objection, latent or expressed: could the kingdom really grow from such inauspicious beginnings? His reply was that the little cell of disciples would indeed become a kingdom. And, in the last analysis, if the kingdom does reach its full dimension, that is not due to anything in the men and women who are the seed of the kingdom; the growth is due solely to the power of God. This is why Jesus could speak with utter confidence of the final stage of the kingdom. And that is why both parables are a call for openness and for patience.

Conclusion 4:33-34

In parabolic speech Jesus reveals the kingdom, but his listeners must have ears to hear (vv 9, 13, 23). Those who do hear leave themselves open to the word of God revealed in the word and person of Jesus. If he did explain fully to the insider group of disciples it will be clear throughout the gospel that they failed to understand. They did not really have ears to hear.

A Group of Miracle Stories 4:35–5:43

Who Then is This? 4:35-41

35On that day, when evening had come, he said to them, 'Let us go across to **the other side**.' 36And leaving the crowd behind, they took him with them in the boat, just as he was. Other boats were with him. 37A great windstorm arose, and the waves beat into the boat, so that the boat was already being swamped. 38But he was in the stern, asleep on the cushion; and they woke him up and said to him, 'Teacher, do you not care that we are perishing?'
39He woke up and rebuked the wind and said to the sea, 'Peace! Be still!' Then the wind ceased, and there was a dead calm. 40He said to them, 'Why are you afraid? Have you still no faith?' 41And they were filled with great awe and said to one another, 'Who then is this, that even the wind and the sea obey him?'

It is the evening of the day of parables (see 4:1-2). 'Let us go across to the other side': from now on there will be a frequent criss-crossing of the lake, a going to and fro between the western Jewish shore and the eastern Gentile territory. We shall see that this is a symbolic knitting together of Jew and Gentile in Christian fellowship.

	Lake Crossing in Mark. *Eis to peran* ('to the other side')	

At 4:35 we have the beginning of a series of 'voyages' to and from the western (Jewish) side of the lake [W] to the eastern (Gentile) side [E]:

4:35	Across to the other side – *eis to peran*	E
5:1	Came to the other side	E
5:21	To the other side	W
	[6:32 To a deserted place] (W)]	
6:45	To the other side (Bethsaida)	E
6:53	Crossed over (to Gennesaret)	W
7:31	Land journey to Decapolis	E
8:10	Boat journey to Dalmanutha	W
8:13	To the other side (Bethsaida 8:22)	E
8:27	Caesarea Philippi	N
9:30	Galilee (Capernaum 9:33)	W

The narrative vv 37-41 is a miracle story arranged in three scenes. The first contrasts the plight of the storm-tossed boat with the tranquil sleep of Jesus (vv 37-38a). The second contrasts the abject terror of these professional fishermen with the sovereign calm of Jesus who commands wind and waves with authority (vv 38b-39). In the third place, we are shown the reaction of the disciples to Jesus: they are awe-struck by his display of cosmic power (v 41).

We need to have in mind that certain Old Testament ideas and passages form the background of the narrative. Control over the sea and the calming of storms are characteristic signs of divine power (Job 7:12; Pss 74:13; 89:8-9; 93:3-4; Is 51:9-10). Calming of a storm at sea is a major proof of God's loving care (Ps 107:23-32). It is also noteworthy that peaceful and untroubled sleep is a sign of perfect trust in God (see Prov 3:23-24; Pss 3:5; 4:8; Job 11:18-19). Of particular interest is the passage in Jonah (1:4-15) which seems to have influenced the shape of the Marcan story.

The reproach of v 40 transforms the miracle story into a catechetical lesson; though from the beginning, doubtless, the episode was one which raised the question of the identity of Jesus, and was a teaching on faith. Jesus blames the disciples for their lack of confidence. The term *deiloi*, 'afraid', is very strong, expressing total disarray. During the storm the disciples had failed in that trust in God of which the tranquil sleep of Jesus was a visible sign. He accuses them especially of lack of confidence in him. In their first address to Jesus in this gospel the disciples call him 'Teacher' – a far cry from his true identity as Messiah and Son of God (1:1, 11). Though they have seen Jesus' authority over wind and sea, they have failed to perceive in it the presence of God's kingdom among them. They fail to recognise Jesus, and will persist in their blindness.

Mark looks beyond the little handful of disciples in that lake drama. The cry, 'Teacher, do you not care that we are perishing?' (v 38), suggests that the disciples are in a danger which does not threaten their Master. This scene where the disciples are awake and in danger while their Lord 'sleeps' reflects the post-Easter experience of the church. Christians may feel that the Lord has no care for them, has abandoned them, and the church may seem to be at the mercy of the forces pitted against it. Individuals and communities who feel so earn the rebuke: 'Have you still no faith?' It is enough that he should 'awaken', that they should have faith and trust in his presence, for the storm of their faith to be stilled. Jesus exhorts his disciples to have trust in him at all times and in all circumstances.

An Opening to the Gentiles 5:1-20

[1]They came to **the other side** of the sea, to the country of the Gerasenes. [2]And when he had stepped out of the boat, immediately a man out of the tombs with an unclean spirit met him. [3]He lived among the tombs; and no one could restrain him any more, even with a chain, [4]for he had often been restrained with shackles and chains, but the chains he wrenched apart, and the shackles he broke in pieces; and no one had the strength to subdue him. [5]Night and day among the tombs and on the mountains he was always howling and bruising himself with stones. [6]When he saw Jesus from a distance, he ran and bowed down before him; [7]and he shouted at the top of his voice, 'What have you to do with me, Jesus, Son of the Most High God? I adjure you by God, do not torment me.' [8]For he had said to him, 'Come out of the man, you unclean spirit!' [9]Then Jesus asked him, 'What is your name?' He replied, 'My name is Legion, for we are many.' [10]He begged him earnestly not to send them out of the country.

[11]Now there on the hillside a great herd of swine was feeding; [12]and the unclean spirits begged him, 'Send us into the swine; let us enter them.' [13]So he gave them permission. And the unclean spirits came out and entered the swine; and the herd, numbering about two thousand, rushed down the steep bank into the sea, and were drowned in the sea.

[14]The swineherds ran off and told it in the city and in the country.

Then people came to see what it was that had happened. [15]They came to Jesus and saw the demoniac sitting there, clothed and in his right mind, the very man who had had the legion; and they were afraid. [16]Those who had seen what had happened to the demoniac and to the swine reported it. [17]Then they began to beg Jesus to leave their neighbourhood.

[18]As he was getting into the boat, the man who had been possessed by demons begged him that he might be with him. [19]But Jesus refused, and said to him, 'Go home to your friends, and tell them how much the Lord has done for you, and what mercy he has shown you.' [20]And he went away and began to proclaim in the Decapolis how much Jesus had done for him; and everyone was amazed.

The narrative is smoothly linked to the preceding one (5:1); after the stilling of the storm the boat completes its journey. This story is skilfully presented as a little drama in four acts. The interest shifts from the afflicted man (vv 1-10), to the herd of swine (vv 11-13), then to the people of the area (vv 14-17), and back again to the man and Jesus by the lakeside (vv 18-20). The core of 5:1-20 is an exorcism story which has been embellished with folkloristic details. It can readily be seen that the episode of the swine is not essential to the main story. For the evangelist, however, the resultant dramatic narrative was full of meaning. For this was no ordinary exorcism. The man was victim of an unusually severe case of demonic possession (v 9) – in our terms, he was violently insane. All goes to demonstrate the overweening power of Jesus which not only rid the man of his evil guests, but cleansed the land of them (vv 10-13). The afflicted one's fellow citizens were witnesses to the extraordinary power that had been at work (vv 14-17). The exorcism had taken place in Gentile territory (Decapolis); in this land, cleansed by Jesus himself, the healed man became a precursor, heralding the preaching of the good news to the Gentiles (vv 18-20).

The descriptive passage 5:3-5 carries the stamp of Mark's vocabulary. Its vividness serves to underline the importance of the incident. The demoniac 'bowed down' before Jesus: the evil spirit was conscious of an exceptional spiritual force. In the story line, invocation of the name 'Jesus, Son of the Most High God' (v 7) was probably a despairing attempt to counter the power of the exorcist. It was the evangelist's view, however, that demons, with preternatural insight, perceived something of the true standing of Jesus. 'The Most High

God', a Gentile designation of the God of Israel (see Dan 3:26; Acts 16: 17), came fittingly from a Gentile demon. 'I adjure you by God' was a formula employed in Jewish exorcisms; there is irony in its use here by a demon in addressing Jesus. 'Do not torment me' (v 7) – Matthew (8:29) has caught the implication: 'Have you come to torment us before the time?' The unclean spirit recognised that definitive torment awaited it.

The tables were turned on the demon: Jesus demanded to know its name and won an instant response (v 9). 'Legion' implies that a host of demons had invaded the man. In line with the view that illness was due to evil influences, it is understandable that, popularly, it was believed that a person so fearsomely insane must have been assaulted by a very regiment of baneful forces. Other examples of possession by more than one demon are: Lk 8:2; Mt 12:45; (Mk 16:). Demons, in popular opinion, were thought to be attached to a particular locality from which they were reluctant to be banished; see Lk 11:24. Here, the demon had surrendered and was now pleading desperately for terms (Mk 5:10). The episode of the pigs is patently folk narrative with typical earthy humour. The demons had, seemingly, won a concession, but it proved to be their undoing. We are to take it that they perished with the pigs. No Jew would have shed a tear over the destruction of a herd of pigs – fitting habitat for demons indeed! For Mark the drowning was important as he shows his reader that the episode went far beyond the deliverance of the unhappy possessed one. It was expulsion of a horde of demons from the land, a veritable victory of Jesus in the domain of Satan.

The scene changes (vv 14-20). It is not surprising (as the narrative runs) that the herdsmen fled, nor that people hastened to verify their startling story. The newcomers were filled with superstitious terror of Jesus' awesome power. The contrast of v 15 with vv 3-5 is typical of exorcism stories: the contrast between the violence and destructiveness of the demonic spirit and the tranquillity of the liberated person. The concluding verses 18-20 are theologically eloquent for Mark. The man begged that he 'might be with' Jesus, that he might become a disciple. Jesus' refusal of the man's generous gesture made in thankfulness was by no means ungracious; but discipleship results from the initiative of Jesus. For that matter, it was not wholly a refusal. He would not take the man with him in his immediate circle of disciples because he had a special mission for him; he was to be the first missionary to the Gentiles. And that is why, though the man was bidden to *tell* what *God* had done for him (v 19), what he in fact did was to *'proclaim'* (see 1:14; 3:14) the deed of *Jesus*. The notion of the Christian message to the Gentiles is close to the surface.

Your Faith Has Saved You 5:21-43

[21]When Jesus had crossed again in the boat to **the other side**, a great crowd gathered around him; and he was by the sea. [22]Then one of the leaders of the synagogue named Jairus came and, when he saw him, fell at his feet [23]and begged him repeatedly, 'My little daughter is at the point of death. Come and lay your hands on her, so that she may be **made well and live**.' [24]So he went with him.

And a large crowd followed him and pressed in on him. [25]Now there was a woman who had been suffering from haemorrhages for twelve years. [26]She had endured much under many physicians, and had spent all that she had; and she was no better, but rather grew worse. [27]She had heard about Jesus, and came up behind him in the crowd and touched his cloak, [28]for she said, 'If I but touch his clothes, I will be **made well**.' [29]Immediately her haemorrhage stopped; and she felt in her body that she was **healed of her disease**. [30]Immediately aware that power had gone forth from him, Jesus turned about in the crowd and said, 'Who touched my clothes?' [31]And his disciples said to him, 'You see the crowd pressing in on you; how can you say, "Who touched me?"' [32]He looked all around to see who had done it. [33]But the woman, knowing what had happened to her, came in fear and trembling, fell down before him, and told him the whole truth. [34]He said to her, 'Daughter, your **faith has made you well**; go in peace, and be **healed of your disease**.'

[35]While he was still speaking, some people came from the leader's house to say, 'Your daughter is dead. Why trouble the teacher any further?' [36]But overhearing what they said, Jesus said to the leader of the synagogue, 'Do not fear, only believe.' [37]He allowed no one to follow him except **Peter, James, and John**, the brother of James. [38]When they came to the house of the leader of the synagogue, he saw a commotion, people weeping and wailing loudly. [39]When he had entered, he said to them. 'Why do you make a commotion and weep? The child is not dead but sleeping.' [40]And they laughed at him. Then he put them all outside, and took the child's father and mother and those who were with him, and went in where the child was. [41]He took her by the hand and said to her, 'Talitha cum,' which means, 'Little girl, **get up**!' [42]And immediately the girl **got up** and began to walk about (she was twelve years of age). At this they were overcome with amazement. [43]He strictly ordered them that no one should know this, and he told them to give her something to eat.

The dovetailing of one story with another – his 'sandwich' technique – is a feature of Mark's style. Nowhere else does an insertion so clearly separate two parts of a narrative as it does in 5:21-43 (21-24a [24b-34] 35-43). Each 'sandwich' of Mark is a carefully constructed unit and should be read as such. Here the stories are interwoven to emphasise the same point in each. The closing words of the first part of the daughter of Jairus story (v 24) prepare the way for the story of the woman, and the words, 'while he was still speaking' (v 35), form a neat link with the second part of the main story. It is noteworthy that in these stories two women hold centre stage.

Mark sets the scene on the western shore of the lake after Jesus had crossed over to 'the other side' (v 21). A great crowd by the lakeside is typical (see 3:8-9; 4:1). The suppliant, Jairus, was an *archisynagógos*, director of synagogue worship. Personal dignity forgotten, in his sorrow and concern he fell at the feet of Jesus (see 7:25). The little girl was at the point of death, already beyond any earthly help. In these narratives the raising of the dead girl and the cure of the woman are accomplished through physical contact with Jesus; here the father requests Jesus to impose his hands on the girl. 'That she may be made well (*sózó*) and live (*zaó*)' (v 23). At the catechetical level of the story the words mean: 'That she may be saved and have (eternal) life.' Jesus set out at once with Jairus. Mention of the thronging crowd prepares the way for the story of the woman.

The Woman
The encounter with a troubled woman gives us a precious glimpse of the courtesy of Jesus. On the way to Jairus' home he had sensed that a person of faith had invoked his healing power, by touching his cloak. He asked, 'Who touched my clothes?' His blunt disciples looked at him, pityingly: he was thronged by a crowd and complained that someone had touched him! Jesus knew who that someone was: a woman. A woman, moreover, who suffered from a chronic haemorrhage and was, therefore, ritually unclean. She had no business being in a crowd and, by touching Jesus, rendered him ritually unclean also; or so others would have reckoned. While, for her, the social consequences were not as grave as for the unfortunate leper (1:40-41), she was obliged to live in quiet isolation. Jesus had no patience with such restrictive purity regulations. Later, (v

41) he took by the hand a young woman (twelve years of age) – a gesture inappropriate for a religious leader. He was concerned with people, intent on liberation from physical and social suffering. Jesus did not scold the woman for her 'reprehensible' conduct. Instead, he commended her faith. And he made a point, not only of speaking gently to her, but of addressing her, respectfully, as 'Daughter', that is, daughter of Abraham and Sarah, a child of God. This moving encounter is highlighted by the bracket phrase, 'healed of her disease' (vv 29, 34).

Raising the Dead

To our way of thinking, raising the dead is simply not on: there really is no place for it in our culture. In contrast, many of Jesus' day would have regarded the matter more sympathetically and have been prepared to accept that a holy man might raise the dead to life. For Jews there were the parallel stories of Elijah (1 Kings 17:17-24) and Elisha (2 Kings 4:18-37). As for the gospels, besides Mk 5:21-43, and parallels, we have Lk 7:11-17 and Jn 11:1-46 – the raising, respectively, of the daughter of Jairus, the son of the widow of Nain, and Lazarus. Despite this spread, the basic question is: are these stories creations of the early church, or may they spring from events in the life of Jesus? It surely is not without significance that the other evangelists show no awareness of the Nain (Luke) and Lazarus (John) stories.

Our concern is the raising of the daughter of Jairus. Whatever did occur, it looks as though Mark regarded it as a raising from the dead. Still, there is the observation of Jesus, 'The child is not dead but sleeping' (v 41). This might indicate his more perceptive diagnosis: the child was in a coma, not dead as others thought (see 9:26). A number of factors combine to suggest that the Jairus story ultimately goes back to an incident in the life of the historical Jesus. The story might well be seen as dramatisation of the life-giving power of Jesus.

Furthermore, the evangelist lets it be understood that the narrative of the daughter of Jairus is a manifestation of the power of the risen Lord. Jesus said to the girl: 'Little girl, get up! (arise)'. And immediately the girl got up (arose).

The verbs 'to arise' (*egeirein*) and 'to rise up' (*anistémi*) are used of the resurrection of Jesus (14:28; 16:6 and 8:31; 9:9-10; 10:34). Confirmation of the theological importance of the raising accomplished by Jesus is the exclusive presence of the three privileged witnesses, Peter, James, and John (5:37), who were also alone with Jesus at the transfiguration (9:2), in Gethsemane (14:3) and (with Andrew) on the Mount of Olives as hearers of the farewell discourse (13:3). Each time their presence is a pointer to the reader: here is something especially significant. Jesus raises the dead girl to life because he is 'the resurrection and the life' (Jn 11:25). For Mark and his readers he is the Lord, source of saving power (5:30) and the narrative is a lesson in salvation through faith.

Salvation and faith are, indeed, the major themes of our twin narrative. Jairus was confident that at Jesus' touch his daughter would be 'made well' (v 23) and the woman is persuaded that if she were to touch Jesus' garments she would be 'made well' (v 28). Each time the verb is *sózó* which means also 'to save'. Jairus had pleaded that his daughter may be made well 'and live'. The verb *zaó*, 'to live', had taken on, in Christian usage, overtones of living to eternal life. The plea might be read: 'That she may be saved and have eternal life.' More pointedly, in v 34, Jesus reassured the woman, telling her, 'Your faith has made you well – has saved you.' Mark had in mind more than bodily healing. Salvation stands in close relationship to faith. Jesus, then, exhorted the father of the dead girl, 'Do not fear , only believe' (v 36).

Faith comes to fulfilment in personal encounter with Jesus, in dialogue with him. Jairus believed that Jesus had power to heal one on the point of death (v 23). Jesus looked for a deeper faith: faith in him as one who could raise from the dead, a faith finding expression in the midst of unbelief (vv 35-36). The woman, too, had faith in the power of Jesus (vv 27-28). She, too, was asked to have a fuller faith in him; she met his gaze and came to kneel at his feet (v 33). And, through faith in Jesus, she and the girl were made well – saved. The Christian is asked to recognise that faith in Jesus can transform life and is victory over death. This faith is not something vague or impersonal. One must kneel at his feet, not abjectly, but in the intensity of one's pleading (v 22) or in humble thankfulness (v 33). This Jesus will give to one who believes that peace the world cannot give (v 34). He will assure that person of life beyond death (v41).

A Prophet Without Honour 6:1-6a

> [1]He left that place and came to his hometown, and his disciples followed him. [2]On the sabbath he began to teach in the synagogue, and many who heard him were astounded. They said, 'Where did this man get all this? What is this wisdom that has been given to him? What deeds of power are being done by his hands! [3]Is not this the carpenter, the son of Mary and brother of James and Joses and Judas and Simon, and are not his sisters here with us?' And they took offence at him. [4]Then Jesus said to them, 'Prophets are not without honour, except in their hometown, and among their own kin, and in their own house. [5]And he could do no deed of power there, except that he laid his hands on a few sick people and cured them. [6a]And he was amazed at their unbelief.

The episode of the rejection of Jesus at Nazareth (6:1-6a) had deep meaning for Mark and he placed it deliberately at this point in his gospel. A poignant problem in the early days of the church was the fact that while many Gentiles were responding to the good news, the Jewish people resisted it (see Rom 9-11).

Already, in Mark, the bitter opposition of the authorities to Jesus has been demonstrated (2:1–3:6) and he was shown as misunderstood by his own family (3:20-35). Now, at the close of the Galilean mission, his own townspeople were challenged to make up their minds about his person and his claims, and they took offence at him. Their rejection of him was an anticipation of his rejection by the Jewish nation (15:11-15). That final rejection was possible because the blindness of people to God's revelation had been present from the start (see Jn 1:10-11). The issue is one of faith or unfaith in Jesus. Or, in Christian terms, faith in or rejection of the Lord.

The passage lays bare one of the roots of unbelief. Jesus' townsfolk reacted with initial surprise. They wondered at the origin ('where') of his wisdom; they had heard of his 'deeds of power'. But they made the mistake of imagining that they already had the answers to their own questions. Besides, there was the scandal of Jesus' ordinariness: they could not bring themselves to acknowledge the greatness or the mission of a man who was one of themselves.

'He could do no deed of power there': Jesus' healings were always done in an atmosphere of faith; there was no context of faith in his hometown. The healing of a few sick people (v 5) is evidently not regarded as miraculous.

They 'took offence' at him: by Mark's day *skandalon* had practically become a technical term to designate the obstacle which some found in Christ and which blocked them from passing to Christian faith and discipleship (see Rom 9:32-33; 1 Cor 1:23; 1 Peter 2:8). The proverb of v 4 – 'Prophets are not without honour, except in their hometown ...' – in some form was current in the ancient world. Jesus implicitly assumed the role of prophet. His word must have consoled the early church in face of the enigmatic refusal of the chosen people as a whole to accept the message of Jesus. Christian communities down the ages would have done well to have taken it to heart. Prophets are never comfortable people to have about and we are adept at finding ways of discrediting them.

C. Jesus and the Disciples 6:6b–8:30

⁶ᵇThen he went about the villages teaching.

⁷He called the twelve and began to send them out two by two, and gave them authority over the unclean spirits. ⁸He ordered them to take nothing for their journey except a staff; no bread, no bag, no money in their belts; ⁹but to wear sandals, and not to put on two tunics. ¹⁰He said to them, 'Wherever you enter a house, stay there until you leave the place. ¹¹If any place will not welcome you and they refuse to hear you, as you leave, shake off the dust that is on your feet as a testimony against them.' ¹²So they went out and proclaimed that all should repent. ¹³They cast out many demons, and anointed with oil many who were sick and cured them.

¹⁴King Herod heard of it, for Jesus' name had become known. Some were saying, 'John the baptiser has been raised from the dead; and for this reason these powers are at work in him.' ¹⁵But others said, 'It is Elijah.' And others said, 'It is a prophet, like one of the prophets of old.' ¹⁶But when Herod heard of it, he said, 'John, whom I beheaded, has been raised.'

¹⁷For Herod himself had sent men who arrested John, bound him, and put him in prison on account of Herodias, his brother Philip's wife, because Herod had married her. ¹⁸For John had been telling Herod, 'It is not lawful for you to have your brother's wife.' ¹⁹And Herodias had a grudge against him, and wanted to kill him. But she could not. ²⁰For Herod feared John, knowing that he was a righteous and holy man, and he protected him. When he heard him, he was greatly perplexed; and yet he liked to listen to him.

²¹But an opportunity came when Herod on his birthday gave a banquet for his courtiers and officers and for the leaders of Galilee. ²²When his daughter Herodias came in and danced, she pleased Herod and his guests; and the king said to the girl, 'Ask me whatever you wish, and I will give it.' ²³And he solemnly swore to her, 'Whatever you ask me, I will give you, even half of my kingdom.' ²⁴She went out and said to her mother, 'What should I ask for?' She replied, 'The head of John the baptiser.' ²⁵Immediately she rushed back to the king and requested, 'I want you to give me at once the head of John the Baptist on a platter.' ²⁶The king was deeply grieved; yet out of regard for his oaths and for the guests, he did not want to refuse her. ²⁷Immediately the king sent a soldier of the guard with orders to bring John's head. He went and beheaded him in the

prison, [28]brought his head on a platter, and gave it to the girl. Then
the girl gave it to her mother. [29]When his disciples heard about it,
they came and took his body, and laid it in a tomb.
[30]The apostles gathered around Jesus, and told him all that they had
done and taught.

This section begins with the mission of the Twelve and closes with
the confession of Peter at Caesarea Philippi, and the disciples figure
prominently throughout. But, apart from the opening and closing
episodes, the emphasis is on their lack of understanding, which
becomes more and more pronounced. And the evangelist does
show considerable interest in the Gentile mission which must,
therefore, be regarded as a major theme. At any rate, this unit, like
the previous two, begins with a summary statement of the activity
(teaching) of Jesus (6:6b) and concludes with the adoption of an attitude towards him (8:27-29).

Mission of the Twelve 6:[6b]7-13

Jesus has been rejected by his own people. Now he turns his attention to the Twelve. He had chosen them 'to be with him' (3:14) and
he had concentrated on instructing them. But he had chosen them
too, 'to be sent out to proclaim the message'; the time has come for
them to take an active part in the mission. The are given authority
over unclean spirits; up until now Jesus alone exercised this authority. The disciples now share in the mission of Jesus. Yet, Mark carefully avoids stating, unlike Matthew and Luke (see Mt 10:7; Lk 9:2),
that they proclaimed the kingdom. In his perspective the disciples
have not yet understood the true nature of the kingdom. Like the
Baptist, they preached 'that all should repent' (v 12).

The brief summary (v 6b) is transitional: Jesus makes another cir-
cuit of the villages of Galilee (see 1:38-39; 5:14; 6:56). The sending
out of the disciples 'two by two' follows Jewish practice. They are to
take nothing with them for the journey. During their visit to a village they will remain in the house where they first found hospitality
and not move to more congenial quarters. 'Shake off the dust that is
on your feet': a symbolic action indicating that the place is as good
as heathen. Jews shook off heathen dust on re-entering Palestine.
'As a testimony against them,' that is, as a warning: the gesture is
intended to make them think again and lead them to repentance.

In a summarising passage (vv 12-13), Mark's reference to the

preaching of repentance is deliberate: in his plan the preaching of
the imminence of the kingdom is reserved to Jesus; the disciples,
like the Baptist, prepare for Jesus' proclamation. They did share in
the exorcising and healing work of Jesus. Oil was used in medical
treatment (see Lk 10:34). If the disciples do now share in the mission
of Jesus, it is only in association with Jesus can their mission pros-
per. They will learn to their cost (see 9:14-29) that apart from him
they can do nothing (Jn 15:5).

The Death of John the Baptist 6:14-29

Between the sending of the Twelve (vv 7-13) and their return (v 30)
Mark has, in customary fashion, inserted another episode: the
death of the Baptist. The shadow of the cross falls starkly across the
gospel because the death of the precursor is a presage of Jesus' fate.

'Herod' is Herod Antipas, son of Herod the Great, and tetrarch of
Galilee. He had heard a report of the disciples' activity throughout
Galilee (v 12), which had given a boost to the renown of Jesus (v 14).
There were various opinions as to who Jesus himself might be: John
the Baptist *redivivus*, Elijah, a prophet. Later, in 8:28, these popular
opinions are again listed. Herod is said to have shared the naïve
view which identified Jesus with a Baptist restored to life (v 16).

The story of the Baptist's execution (vv 17-29) is the only narrative
in Mark which is not directly a story about Jesus. Yet it, too, is concerned with him, for it aims to present John as a precursor whose
death prefigured the death of Jesus (see 9:11-13). The story has been
coloured by reminiscences of Old Testament precedents. One can
think of Jezebel, who sought Elijah's death (1 Kings 19:2). Then, the
influence of the book of Esther is undoubted. This is rather surprising because the characters do not correspond. It may be that in this
popular and vivid tale of the Baptist's death reminiscences of
Jezebel and Esther are involuntary rather than studied.

There are notable differences between Mark's account of the death
of the Baptist and that of the Jewish historian Flavius Josephus in
his *Antiquities*. According to Josephus, John was imprisoned in the
fortress of Machaerus on the east of the Dead Sea and was put to
death there. Mark gives the impression that the scene of the banquet (and so of the death of John) was Herod's Galilean capital of
Tiberias. Josephus alleges a political motive for John's imprison-

ment and execution. For Mark, the motivation is John's denunciation of the open adultery of Antipas and Herodias before their divorces and marriage, which aroused the implacable hatred of Herodias. It is noteworthy that the differences between Mark and Josephus centre on the theme of the banquet and the role of Herodias and so stem mostly from the parallelism of the Marcan story with the stories of Jezebel and Esther. The explanation seems to be that Mark has woven colourful and legendary details into his broadly historical narrative of the fate of John the Baptist.

Imprisonment of John was not enough for Herodias; like Jezebel who engineered the death of Naboth (1 Kgs 21), she plotted his death. Antipas' attitude to John is remarkably like that of Ahab to Elijah (1 Kgs 21:17-29). He seized the opportunity of meeting his prisoner and heard him with mixed feelings.

Herodias bided her time and her chance came on Herod's birthday. Antipas' banquet is like that of Ahasuerus (Xerxes), who 'gave a banquet for all his princes and servants' (Esther 1:12). Herodias' daughter 'pleased Herod' – cf Est 2:9: 'And the maiden Esther pleased him.' The king's offer is a familiar feature of such stories. Cf Est 5:3: 'And the king said to her, What is it, Queen Esther? What is your request? It shall be given to you, even to the half of my kingdom.' The delighted girl sought her mother's advice and Herodias grasped her chance without hesitation; the execution was carried out on the spot. 'He went and beheaded him'; compare the terse word of Jesus' execution, 'and they crucified him' (Mk 15:24) – in each case the grim event is described as starkly as possible. The Baptist's disciples (see 2:18) see to his burial. 'His body', literally 'corpse' (*ptóma*) – in 15:45 the same word is used of the body of Jesus. But there the resemblance ends. The disciples of Jesus had fled (14:50); another had buried his body (15:43-46). The passion of the precursor ended in death, that of the Messiah in resurrection.

The Return of the Disciples 6:30
The disciples who had been sent out – this is the straightforward meaning of the designation 'apostles' here – now return. Though sent by Jesus to share his mission, they now excitedly report 'all' that they had done and what they had taught. They had forgotten that they had been empowered by him. The disciples 'come back flushed with their success, yet show that they have failed as disci-

ples of Jesus. Mark has already portrayed the disciples' inability to understand *who Jesus is* in 4:35-41 (see 4:41). In 6:7-30, he further shows that they have difficulty in grasping *who they are.'* (F. J. Moloney, *The Gospel of Mark,* Hendrickson , 2002, 129).

The arrangement of 6:32–8:26

Any endeavour to understand Mark must take seriously his arrangement of his material. We should note, then, that the episodes of 6:32–8:26 are ordered in two parallel series of events:

Feeding of the 5000 (6:35-44)	Feeding of the 4000 (8:1-9)
Crossing of the Lake (6:45-56)	Crossing of the Lake (8:10)
Controversy with Pharisees (7:1-23)	Controversy with Pharisees (8:11-13)
The Children's Bread (7:24-30)	The One Loaf (8:14-21)
Healing of a Deaf Mute (7:31-37)	Healing of a Blind Man (8:22-26)

The first multiplication of loaves takes place in Galilee and its beneficiaries are Jews. Moreover, the number twelve (6:43) evokes the twelve tribes of Israel. But the second feeding takes place, according to Mark, in Decapolis (see 7:31), that is, in largely pagan territory. One may assume that, this time, those who benefit from the miracle are Gentiles. Following on the Jews, the Gentiles too are called to share in the feeding, a prefiguration of the eucharistic meal and the messianic banquet.

The Bread of the Banquet

All four gospels carry the story of the multiplication of loaves: Mark (6:32-44; 8:1-10) and Matthew (14:13-21; 15:29-38) have two accounts of a miraculous feeding. There are several arguments for regarding these two accounts in Mark and Matthew as variant forms of the same incident. Luke (9:10-17) follows Mark 6:32-44. It seems best to take it that the fourth evangelist (John 6:1-15) drew on an independent tradition like that of Mark's and Matthew's second version.

In the teaching tradition of the Christian community the relevance of the multiplication of loaves to the eucharist, the bread of God's people, was quickly recognised. We find close parallels in gesture and wording between both synoptic accounts and the narratives of the Last Supper. 'While they were eating, he took a loaf of bread, and after blessing it he broke it, and gave it to them ...' (14:22). Compare: 'Taking the five loaves ... he blessed and broke the loaves, and gave ...' (6:41); 'He took the seven loaves ... and after giving thanks he broke them and gave ...' (8:6). And it was only at the feeding miracle and the Last Supper that Jesus explicitly acted as host of a meal. John's account, too, shows some adaptation (Jn 6: 4-14). And, of course, in his plan, the multiplication of loaves was the starting point of the Bread of Life discourses. It is evident, then, that the story of the feeding was treasured in the early communities not only because it related a mighty work of Jesus, but also because of its symbolic relation to the eucharist.

The story of Jesus feeding the multitude has association not only with the eucharist but also with a meal pattern throughout the ministry. Matthew 11:18-19 sets up a contrast between the Baptist and Jesus: 'John came neither eating nor drinking ... the Son of man came eating and drinking, and they say, "Look, a glutton and a drunkard, a friend of tax collectors and sinners!"' The saying presupposes a well-established reputation. Jesus, unlike the Baptist, was no ascetic. This squares with Jesus' contention that, as long as he was with them, his disciples cannot fast (Mk 2:19). Reference to tax collectors and sinners is important. Jesus showed his concern for the socially despised and for 'sinners' (non-observant Jews on a par with Gentiles) precisely through table fellowship with them. Thus, in Mk 2:16, the challenge of the Pharisees to the disciples, 'Why does he eat with tax collectors and sinners?' and the note of exasperation, if not of disgust, in Lk 15:2: 'And the Pharisees and the scribes were grumbling, and saying, "This fellow welcomes sinners and eats with them!"'

We may find the key to Jesus' understanding of his practice of table fellowship with outcasts in Mt 8:11: 'I tell you, many will come from east and west and will eat with Abraham and Isaac and Jacob in the kingdom of heaven' (see Lk 13:28). His shared meals were a preparation for and an anticipation of the final banquet in the kingdom.

Moreover, in table fellowship with sinners Jesus was displaying the Father's preferential option for sinners (see Lk 15:7, 10). If, then, at the Last Supper, Jesus asserted that his next drink of wine would be at table in the fullness of the kingdom, he implied that the Supper was the climax of a series of meals which celebrated, in anticipation, the joy of the banquet. They were meals which, indeed, opened the banquet to all who would not deliberately reject the invitation. It is against this rich background we may expect to understand the story of the feeding. The view of John P. Meier is persuasive:

> It is within this greater context and regular habit of Jesus' public ministry, a habit that culminated with what was literally the Last Supper among a great number of 'suppers', that one may try to understand the origin of the story of the feeding miracle. In my opinion, the criterion of both multiple attestation and coherence make it likely that, amid the various celebrations of table fellowship Jesus hosted during his ministry, there was one especially memorable one: memorable because of the unusual number of participants, memorable also because, unlike many meals held in towns and villages, this one was held by the Sea of Galilee. In contrast to Jesus' other 'kingdom meals', bread and fish rather than bread and wine (cf Mt 11:18-19 par; Mk 14:22-25) would be the natural components of such a meal at such a spot. Connected from the beginning with Jesus' eschatological message, this special meal of bread and fish, shared by a large crowd by the Sea of Galilee, would be remembered and interpreted by the post Easter church through the filter of the Last Supper tradition and the church's own celebration of the eucharist. (*A Marginal Jew*, Vol 2, New York: Doubleday, 1994, p 966).

Feeding of Five Thousand – in Israel 6:31-44

[31]He said to them, 'Come away to **a deserted place** all by yourselves and rest a while.' For many were coming and going, and they had no leisure even to eat. [32]And they went away in the boat to **a deserted place** by themselves. [33]Now many saw them going and recognised them, and they hurried there on foot from all the towns and arrived ahead of them. [34]As he went ashore, he saw a great crowd; and he had compassion for them, because they were like sheep without a shepherd; and he began to teach them many things. [35]When it grew late, his disciples came to him and said, 'This is **a deserted place**, and the hour is now very late; [36]send them away so that they may

go into the surrounding country and villages and buy something for themselves to eat.' 37But he answered them, 'You give them something to eat.' They said to him, 'Are we to go and buy two hundred denarii worth of bread, and give it to them to eat?' 38And he said to them, 'How many loaves have you?' When they had found out, they said, 'Five, and two fish.' 39Then he ordered them to get all the people to sit down in groups on the green grass. 40So they sat down in groups of hundreds and of fifties. 41**Taking** the five loaves and the two fish, he looked up to heaven, and **blessed** and **broke** the loaves, and **gave** them to his disciples to set before the people; and he divided the two fish among them all. 42And all ate and were filled; 43and they took up twelve baskets full of broken pieces and of the fish. 44Those who had eaten the loaves numbered five thousand men.

The details of 6:31-32 are quite vague and the destination is unknown. It is somewhere on the western shore because, at v 45, they cross 'to the other side, to Bethsaida', on the eastern shore. For the evangelist the important factor is that the disciples reach a 'desert' place – evoking the Exodus and the gift of manna. Jesus' attempt to find solitude for himself and the disciples is frustrated, but he is not annoyed. Instead, he is deeply moved by the earnestness of the crowd and by their need. The image of a shepherdless people is found in Num 27:17; 1 Kgs 22:17. Jesus sees himself in their regard as the messianic shepherd (Ezek 34; Jn 10:1-18) who will feed his sheep (Ezek 34:13-14; Jn 10:9). The motif of the sheep without a shepherd foreshadows the moment when the shepherd will be stricken and his sheep scattered (Mk 14:27). The people's most pressing hunger was spiritual and he began to teach them.

The significance of the desert place begins to emerge (vv 35-36): as a setting for the gift of miraculous bread (vv 41, 44) it recalls the manna (Exod 16:12-35). By question and answer (v 37) Mark surely intends to bring out the disciples' lack of understanding. The desert setting and the good shepherd theme ought (in Mark's eyes) to have inspired them with trust in Jesus' power. Their reply is sarcastic: 'Fine ... but where are we going to get the money?' – a reaction like that of Moses (see Num 11:13, 21-22). The disciples had some provisions, presumably in the boat. The loaves were likely of barley (see Jn 6:9) and the fish cured. There is a striking parallel in 2 Kgs 4:42-44. Elisha had been brought twenty barley loaves. He proposed to feed a hundred men and his servant objected that the available bread was inadequate. Elisha is confident that the Lord will take care.

It was customary for a Jewish host, at the start of a meal, to pronounce a blessing over the bread and then to break it and distribute it to his guests. If the number was large, others would help in the distribution. The disciples do play an active role; Jesus has shown them how to be shepherds. 'Took … blessed … broke … gave' is consciously eucharistic terminology; the agreement with 14:22 is unmistakable. This explains, too, the rather awkward reference to the fish in v 41; because of the eucharistic significance the emphasis is on the loaves; the distribution of the fish is relegated to a parenthesis. In 2 Kgs 4:44 we read, 'And they ate, and had some left, according to the word of the Lord.' Here (v 43) more is left over at the end than was there at the beginning – a greater than Elisha is here. The disciples gathered *klasmata*, (broken pieces of bread); in the early church the term was used of the eucharistic bread. 'Twelve baskets': the number twelve evokes the number of the tribes of Israel. And the Greek *cophinos* was a specifically Jewish word for basket. The story ends without any of the expressions of wonder customary at the close of a miracle story. Mark regards the incident as a messianic sign bearing on the mystery of Jesus' person.

Crossing the Lake:
The Walking on the Sea 6:45-56
45Immediately he made his disciples get into the boat and go on ahead to **the other side**, to Bethsaida, while he dismissed the crowd. 46After saying farewell to them, he went up on the mountain to pray.
47When evening came, the boat was out on the sea, and he was alone on the land. 48When he saw that they were straining at the oars against an adverse wind, he came towards them early in the morning, walking on the sea. He intended to pass them by. 49But when they saw him walking on the sea, they thought it was a ghost and cried out; 50for they all saw him and were terrified. But immediately he spoke to them and said, 'Take heart, it is I; do not be afraid.' 51Then he got into the boat with them and the wind ceased. And they were utterly astounded, 52for they did not understand about the loaves, but their hearts were hardened.
53When they **had crossed over**, they came to land at Gennesaret and moored the boat. 54When they got out of the boat, people at once recognised him, 55and rushed about that whole region and began to

bring the sick on mats to wherever they heard he was. [56]And wherever he went, into villages or cities or farms, they laid the sick in the marketplaces, and begged him that they might touch even the fringe of his cloak; and all who touched it were healed.

The incident of the walking on the lake is closely connected with the feeding of the five thousand in the synoptics (Mk/Mt) and John. 'He made his disciples get into the boat' (v 45) – there is a sense of urgency and constraint. Jesus forces his disciples to cross the lake. He had prepared them for a Gentile mission (see 5:1-20); now he expects them to lead the way. But, as it turns out, they fail, because they had not grasped the significance of a former journey (4:35-41). That Mark does mean to imply a journey to the eastern side of the lake is clear from the phrases 'the other side' (v 45) and 'when they had crossed over' (v 53). 'He went up on the mountain to pray' just as he prayed in 1:35 and 14:35, 39. On both these occasions, as here, the true nature of Jesus' messiahship is involved and he has to contend with the incomprehension of his disciples (1:36-37; 6:52; 14:40).

There is no suggestion of a storm (as in 4:37); the disciples struggled against a headwind. The incident is certainly mysterious. Again (see 4:37-39) we may ask, What really occurred? 'Walking on the sea'; this appearance of Jesus on the waters is reminiscent of the manifest power of Yahweh; see Job 9: 8, '(God) who trampled the waves of the sea'; also, Job 38:16; Ps 77:19; Sirach 24:5. 'He intended to pass them by' – in the Emmaus story of Luke the similar phrase, 'he walked ahead as if he were going on' (Lk 24:28), is meant as a test of the two disciples, with everything depending on whether they would press Jesus to stay with them. Similarly here the disciples' faith is tested. They failed to recognise that the kingdom of God was present in Jesus, in his person, words, and deeds. 'They thought it was a ghost' (see Lk 24:37); the disciples' reaction is part of the theme of misunderstanding. Yet, they were not fancying something, for 'They all saw him.' 'It is I'; the *egó eimi*, in this epiphany context, may have a suggestion of the Johannine 'I am' sayings – his oneness with God (see Exod 3:14; Is41:4).

'Their hearts were hardened' (v 52) is a strong statement, meaning blindness of heart; it is used of the Pharisees in 3:5. The disciples have practically put themselves among 'those outside' (4:11). Their lack of understanding bears on the significance of the feeding; they will fail, too, to grasp the meaning of the other miracle of loaves (see 8:14-21). We shall see that what they have failed to grasp is that Jesus brings about the unity of Jew and Gentile: he is the 'one loaf' for them (8:14). His calming of storm (4:39) and stilling of wind (6:51) were designed to smooth the path to the Gentiles. Because they had not really come to know him (v 49), the disciples did not perceive the universal scope of his mission. If they are 'utterly astounded' it is because they have not yet really understood at all. In this way Mark invites his readers to a salutary reflection on the meaning of the multiplication of loaves.

The passage 6:53-56 is a typical Marcan summary, a generalised description of Jesus' healing activity. However, the first item, the landing (v 53) does establish a connection with the foregoing narratives, for the sequence feeding-crossing-landing is well attested (Mk 6:30-56; 8:1-10; Jn 6:1-25) and is obviously traditional. The summary, as might be expected, has numerous borrowings from and echoes of other Marcan passages.

Controversy with the Pharisees 7: 1-23
He Declared All Foods Clean

   [1]Now when the Pharisees and some of the scribes who had come from Jerusalem gathered around him, [2]they noticed that some of his disciples were eating with defiled hands, that is, without washing them. [3](For the Pharisees, and all the Jews, do not eat unless they thoroughly wash their hands, thus observing the tradition of the elders; [4]and they do not eat anything from the market unless they wash it; and there are also many other traditions that they observe, the washing of cups, pots, and bronze kettles.) [5]So the Pharisees and the scribes asked him, 'Why do your disciples not live according to the traditions of the elders, but eat with defiled hands?'
   [6]He said to them, 'Isaiah prophesied rightly about you hypocrites, as it is written,

   this people honours me with their lips,
   but their hearts are far from me;
   [7]in vain do they worship me,
   teaching human precepts as doctrines.

[8]You abandon the commandment of God and hold to human tradition.
   [9]Then he said to them, 'You have a fine way of rejecting the commandment of God in order to keep your tradition! For Moses said, 'Honour your father and your mother', and, 'Whoever speaks evil

of father or mother must surely die.' [11]But you say that if anyone tells father or mother, 'whatever support you might have had from me is Corban' (that is, an offering to God) – [12]then you no longer permit doing anything for a father or mother, [13]thus making void the word of God through your tradition that you have handed on. And you do many things like this.'

[14]Then he called the crowd again and said to them, 'Listen to me, all of you, and understand: [15]there is nothing outside a person that by going in can defile, but the things that come out are what defile.'

[17]When he had left the crowd and entered the house, his disciples asked him about the parable. [18]He said to them, 'Then do you also fail to understand? Do you not see that whatever goes into a person from outside cannot defile, [19]since it enters, not the heart but the stomach, and goes out into the sewer?' (Thus he declared all foods clean). [20]And he said, it is what comes out of a person that *defiles a person*. [21]For it is from within, from the human heart, that evil intentions come: fornication, theft, murder, [22]adultery, avarice, wickedness, deceit, licentiousness, envy, slander, pride, folly. [23]All these evil things come from within, and they **defile a person**.'

The controversy setting in 7:1-2 is similar to that in 2:8 and 2:23-24. From chapter 5 on Mark has displayed interest in the Gentile mission; we can appreciate that the matter of Jewish observance was an issue for his community. 'The scribes who had come from Jerusalem' (see 3:2) represent the Jewish position. The question to be answered was whether Gentile Christians had to conform to Jewish tradition (see Gal 2; Acts 15). Mark's adaptation of the Jesus tradition served his situation.

As the text stands, a precise incident lay behind Jesus' dispute with the Pharisees and scribes (Mk 7:1-23): they had observed that the disciples of Jesus did not practise the ritual washing of hands before meals. In their eyes this constituted a transgression of the 'tradition of the elders' – the *halakah*, the oral law. These pharisaic traditions claimed to interpret and complete the Mosaic law and were considered equally authoritative and binding. Later rabbis would claim that 'the ancestral law' constituted a second, oral, law given, together with the written law, to Moses on Sinai.

The tradition of the elders 7:6-13

In responding to the charge of neglecting one observance (v 5) Jesus turned the debate on to a wider issue: the relative worth of oral law and Mosaic law. He cited Is 29:13 (in its Greek form!) against the

Pharisees, drawing a parallel between 'human precepts' of which
Isaiah spoke and the 'human tradition' on which the Pharisees
counted. Jesus rejected the oral law because it was the work of men
(not word of God) and because it could and did conflict with the
law of God. The oral law had put casuistry above love. He
instanced (vv 9-13) a glaring example of casuistry run wild: a precise vow of dedication. A man might declare *Korban* – that is, dedi-
cated to God – the property or capital which, by right, should go to
the support of his parents. Property thus made over by vow took on
a sacred character; the parents had no more claim on it. In point of
fact, such a vow was legal fiction, a mean way of avoiding filial
responsibility. But it was a vow and, as such, in rabbinical eyes, was
binding and could not be dispensed. In this manner, a solemn duty,
enjoined by Torah, was set aside. Jesus could multiply examples, he
declared (v 13). He was aware that one whose mind runs to casuistry loses all sense of proportion. Minute detail becomes more and
more important. Law and observance become an obsession. People
are defined in terms of conformity or of 'sinful' departure from it. It
is a disease far worse than miserliness. For the most part, the miser
nurses his own misery. Casuists are regularly in positions of authority
and make life miserable for others – especially the vulnerable.

The new law of purity 7:14-23
The principle of clean and unclean (a strictly ritual principle) was at
the root of Jewish concern with ritual purity. A saying of Jesus
(authentic in light of the criterion of discontinuity – it is out of step
with the currently accepted view) struck at the very distinction of
clean and unclean, of sacred and secular: 'There is nothing outside a
person that by going in can defile, but the things that come out are
what defile' (v 15). At one stroke Jesus had set aside the whole concept of ritual impurity. Holiness does not lie in the sphere of 'clean'
over against 'unclean'; it is not in the realm of *things* but in the realm
of *conduct*. It is to be found in the human heart and is a matter of
human responsibility. Mark's parenthetical comment – 'Thus he
declared all foods clean' (v 19) – correctly caught the nuance of the
saying. It is, more generally, a flat denial that any external things or
circumstances can separate one from God (see Rom 8:38-39). We
can be separated from God only through our own attitude and
behaviour. In a Gentile-Christian setting this saying of v 15 was

provided with a commentary (vv 17-22). The first half – nothing outside a person can defile – is explained in vv 18b-19 and the second part of the verse – it is what comes out of a person that makes one unclean – is developed in vv 20-23.

Lists of sins and vices (vv 21-22) were commonplace in hellenistic popular philosophy. For other similar lists in the New Testament see Gal 5:19-21; Rom 1:29-31; 1 Peter 4:3. In the Greek the first six nouns in Mark's list are in the plural, indicating evil acts: acts of sexual vice, thefts, murders, adulteries, acts of coveting or lust, and wickedness in general. The six following vices are: deceit, wantonness, envy (literally, an 'evil eye'), slander, pride (arrogance), and folly (the stupidity of one who lacks moral judgement). V 23 simply explains the phrase 'what comes out of a person' of v 20. 'All these evil things' are found within oneself; it is these and not anything external to one which defile. That defilement can come only from within is emphasised by the repeated phrase 'defile a person' which brackets the list of sins and vices. In this discussion as a whole (vv 6-23) it was made clear to Gentile Christians that being followers of Christ did not involve them in observance of Jewish practices. 'The Way' (see Acts 9:2; 19:9, 23) is truly open to all men and women.

Jesus' contrast between word of God and human law, and his emphatic assertion of the priority of the former, are obviously of abiding validity and moment. In our day we face a particularly painful instance of a clash of interests. The eucharist is surely central to Christianity. The Christian people of God have a God-given right to the eucharist. Increasingly, the Christian people are being deprived of the eucharist on foot of a man-made regulation: mandatory celibacy. Ideology takes precedence over theology and pastoral concern. What, now, of the challenge of Jesus: 'You abandon the commandment of God and hold to human tradition' (7:8)?

The Gentile Woman 7:24-30
The Children's Bread
    24From there he set out and went away to the region of Tyre. He entered a house and did not want anyone to know he was there. Yet he could not escape notice, 25but a woman whose little daughter had an unclean spirit immediately heard about him, and she came and bowed down at his feet. 26Now the woman was a Gentile, of

> Syrophoenician origin. She begged him to cast the demon out of her
> daughter. [27]He said to her, 'Let the children be fed first, for it is not
> fair to take the children's food and throw it to the dogs.' [28]But she
> answered him, 'Sir, even the dogs under the table eat the children's
> crumbs.' [29]Then he said to her, 'For saying that, you may go – the
> demon has left your daughter.' [30]So she went home, found the child
> lying on the bed, and the demon gone.

'He set out and went' (v 24) – the same statement in 1:35 and 10:1
indicates a new turn to the mission. For Mark the presence of Jesus
in the region of Tyre, a mainly Gentile area bordering on north-
western Galilee, and his healing wrought for a Gentile woman, carried great weight. The focus of the story is the dialogue between
Jesus and the woman; the exorcism is secondary. The saying of
Jesus, 'It is not fair to take the children's food and throw it to the
dogs' (v 27) shows him acknowledging the distinction between Jew
and Gentile. The woman will not be put off by Jesus' refusal: all
very well indeed – but even the dogs get crumbs! And Jesus
responded to the challenge. This quickwitted woman appealed to
his sense of humour. From the vantage point of successful Gentile
mission, Mark had modified the saying by prefacing, 'Let the children (i.e. Jews) be fed first'; in his day the turn of the Gentiles had
come. No longer do they live on crumbs. They, too, are children,
and have a right to the children's bread. This is because Jesus is the
'one loaf' for Jew and Gentile (see 8:14).

The woman was 'a Gentile, of Syrophoenician origin' (v 26) – a
Gentile both by religion and by birth, a representative of the Gentile
world. The suppliant's little daughter had an unclean spirit: Mark's
predilection for exorcism stories. Jesus' refusal (v 27) was cleverly
trumped by the woman (v 28). He bowed to the woman's faith and
assured her that her child was already healed. If Jesus had yielded
to this cry of faith even while the division between Jew and Gentile
still stood (see Eph 2:11-12), how much more, Mark seems to say,
must the Christian church go out to Gentiles now that Jesus had
laid down his life as a ransom 'for many [all]' (Mk 10:45), had
poured out his blood 'for many [all]'.

The indications are that Mark 7:24–8:26 was planned to meet the
interest of Gentile-Christian readers. Mark wanted to show that the
concern of Jesus, despite the constraint of his mission, ('to the lost

sheep of the house of Israel', Mt 15:24), was not limited to Jews but reached to non-Jewish peoples, beyond the confines of Galilee. When one examines the topographical references in 7:24 and 7:31, one finds that it was Mark who engineered this brief venture of Jesus beyond Jewish territory. Apart from this and the Gerasene demoniac episode (5:1-20), Mark has given only an intimation, expressed in terms of journeys across the lake, of a ministry of Jesus to Gentiles.

The Healing of a Deaf Mute 7:31–37
He has Done Everything Well
> ³¹Then he returned from the region of Tyre, and went by way of Sidon towards the Sea of Galilee, **in the region of the Decapolis**. ³²They brought to him a deaf man who had an impediment in his speech, and they begged him to lay his hand on him. ³³He took him aside in private, away from the crowd, and put his fingers into his ears, and he spat and touched his tongue. ³⁴Then looking up to heaven, he sighed and said to him, 'Ephphatha,' that is, 'Be opened.' ³⁵And immediately his ears were opened, his tongue was released, and he spoke plainly. ³⁶Then Jesus ordered them to tell no one; but the more he ordered them, the more zealously they proclaimed it. ³⁷They were astounded beyond measure, saying, 'He has done everything well: he even makes the deaf to hear and the mute to speak.'

Mark has set the healing of a deaf-mute in the Gentile region of Decapolis (east of the Jordan). As in his previous episode (the exorcism of a Gentile woman's daughter), he is concerned with Jesus' attitude to the Gentiles. In that story, the casting out of the unclean spirit which possessed the Gentile girl showed Jesus hearkening to Gentiles and setting them free. This time, in a Gentile setting, a man recovers his faculty of hearing and speaking. The healing has the symbolic intent of showing that the Gentiles, once deaf and dumb towards God, are now capable of hearing God and of rendering him homage. They, too, have become heirs of the eschatological promise to Israel: 'The ears of the deaf will be unstopped … and the tongue of the speechless sing for joy' (Is 35:5-6).

Jesus' actions of putting his fingers into the man's ears and of touching his tongue with spittle, were common to the techniques of Greek and Jewish healers. Here the gestures have a certain 'sacramental' quality (see 8:23). 'Looking up to heaven,' as in 6:41, implies

Jesus' intimacy with God. 'Sigh' expresses his deep sympathy with the sufferer (see 1:41). 'Be opened' – characteristically, Mark translated the Aramaic word *ephphatha*. The description of this cure (v 35) is given solemn cast (the parallel cure in chapter 8 will be described, too, in three clauses [8:25]). Disobedience of the stereotyped injunction to preserve silence is put very strongly (v 36). As in 1:45 the deed was 'proclaimed': the deeds of Jesus cannot but speak the good news. Astonishment was 'beyond measure', the strongest statement of astonishment in Mark; the miracle has exceptional significance. 'He has done everything well' recalls Genesis 1:31. We may also discern in the Greek chorus of the crowd (v 37) the response in faith of the Christian community who perceived in the works of Jesus the time of fulfilment announced by Isaiah.

The bizarre geography reflected in the setting of the story (v 31) is due to theological intent (see 3: 7-8). The 'Sea of Galilee' establishes a link between two places as different as Phoenicia and Decapolis and brings about the global unity of 'Galilee'. This Galilee is a theological place; it is the 'Galilee of the Gentiles' (see Is 9:1-2; Mt 4:12-16). It evokes the call of the Gentiles to salvation. For Mark Galilee has become the place where the gospel of God is heard (1:14-15), where the first disciples are called to become fishers of people (1:17), where the crowds gather from all of ancient Israel (3:7-8), where unity is established between the divided territories (7:31) and where the disciples will be convened to see, again, him who had preached to them there (14:28; 16:7). They will encounter the risen Christ.

Feeding of Four Thousand – Among Gentiles 8: 1-9

[1]In those days when there was again a great crowd without anything to eat, he called his disciples and said to them, [2]'I have compassion for the crowd, because they have been with me now for three days and have nothing to eat. [3]If I send them away hungry to their homes, they will faint on the way – and some of them have come from a great distance.' [4]His disciples replied, 'How can one feed these people with bread here in the desert? [5]He asked them, 'How many loaves do you have?' They said, 'Seven'. [6]Then he ordered the crowd to sit down on the ground; and he **took** the seven loaves, and after **giving thanks** he **broke** them and **gave** them to his disciples to distribute; and they distributed them to the crowd. [7]They had also a few small fish; and after blessing them, he ordered

that these too should be distributed. [8]They ate and were filled; and they took up the broken pieces left over, seven baskets full. [9]Now there were about four thousand people. And he sent them away.

The two Marcan feeding narratives have much in common but also carry some notable differences. Both are set in a 'desert place', the second more explicitly so, and evoke the Exodus and the manna, bread from God. Both, in the description of the miracle (the evangelist does think of miracle), stress the size of the crowd, and food so abundant that a large amount was left over. Both end with the dismissal of the crowd and a journey by boat. We are, beyond doubt, in the presence of a literary doublet. But Mark chose to see two separate incidents. The indications are that he viewed the feeding of the five thousand as a sign to Jews and the feeding of the four thousand as a sign to Gentiles. Already, in 7:27-28 (the encounter with the Syrophoenician woman) there is a plea that the Gentiles, too, be allowed to participate, to a limited extent at least, in God's bounty. But now it is no longer a question of their being permitted to glean crumbs: the disciples are to give them of the abundance of the table (8:8). The debate over the reception of Gentiles into the Christian community is in mind.

The vague introduction 'in those days' is enough for Mark to link this story with the foregoing. No place is mentioned but he evidently is still thinking of the 'region of Decapolis' (7:31). Greater stress is laid on the people's physical hunger (8:1-4) than in 6:34-44; and here (unlike 6:35), Jesus takes the initiative. Here, too, compassion is occasioned by their physical need and not by the fact that they are as sheep without a shepherd who hunger for Jesus' teaching (see 6:34). The 'three days' would seem to be a traditional detail; in the first feeding all took place on one day.

The surprised question of the disciples (v 4) rings strangely after 6:35-44; an indication that we have to do with a literary doublet. Their lack of understanding is again in evidence (see 6:52; 8:19). Here (see 6:35) the setting really is a desert, far from any habitation, a fact which accentuates the Exodus parallel. The form of the question focuses attention on Jesus as the only provider of bread. In v 6 we find the same eucharistic language as in 6:41: took ... giving thanks ... broke ... gave. The only difference is 'giving thanks' (*eucharistein*) in place of 'blessed' (*eulogein*). The term *eulogein* is closer to the

Hebrew *berakah* – the blessing of an object. *Eucharistein* has the sense of 'giving thanks' and soon became the preferred Christian term for the Lord's Supper (see 1 Cor 11:24; Lk 2:19). Here (8:6) the disciples play a more active role (see 6:41). The eucharistic significance is heightened by the care to avoid any mention of the 'few small fish' until after the distribution of the loaves.

In 6:43-44, five thousand had been fed and twelve baskets of the fragments of the bread and fish were collected. In 8:8-9 four thousand were fed and seven baskets of fragments were collected. The differences are obvious but Mark has given us a pointer as to which are, for him, the significant variants: the baskets of fragments (see 8: 19-20). For there is no denying that Mark does strikingly draw attention to the two feeding stories, deliberately repeating the numbers 'twelve' and 'seven' and using again (see 6:43; 8:8) two different words for basket: *cophinos*, a basket commonly used by Jews, and *spyris*, an ordinary basket. 'Twelve' points to Israel; the more universal 'seven' to the Gentiles. Besides, he has insinuated that the first feeding is in a Jewish setting, the other in a Gentile setting (see 7:31). Mark is no careless writer. These details, for him, are meaningful and, in the setting of this section of his gospel (6:35–8:26), we are justified in seeing in them deliberate pointers to Jewish and Gentile components of his Christian community.

Crossing the Lake 8:10
  10And immediately he got into the boat with his disciples and went **to the district of Dalmanutha**.

'And he sent them away' (8:9) – cf 6:45: 'while he dismissed the crowd'. In each case the dismissal is followed by a boat journey across the lake. Dalmanutha is unknown. For Mark, it would seem to be situated on the western shore. Jesus has crossed over from Gentile territory to the land of Israel. There he will come into conflict with Pharisees.

Controversy With Pharisees 8:11-13
  11The Pharisees came and began to argue with him, asking him for a sign from heaven, to test him. 12And he sighed deeply in his spirit and said, 'Why does this generation ask for a sign? Truly I tell you, no sign will be given to this generation'. 13And he left them, and getting into the boat again, he went across to **the other side**.

From 5:35 on we have had one wonder after another, culminating in the 'second' great feeding miracle. For Mark's readers these signs were compelling, and demand for further signs could only reflect sheer perversity. But the scribes had already perversely attributed the exorcising power of Jesus to the prince of demons (3:22). Here the Pharisees play the role of the stubborn 'generation' of Moses' time who so often 'tempted' God by demanding further proofs of his power after he had worked so many signs (see Num 14:11, 22; Deut 1:35). This passage (vv 11-13) is parallel to 4:10 because miracles, like parables, have a deeper level of meaning which can be missed. The Pharisees stand among 'those outside' who will not see. The miracles of Jesus are sign enough – beyond them no sign will be given.

The demand of a 'sign from heaven' is to test Jesus; some apocalyptic portent is envisaged. The Pharisees imagine that their challenge creates a dilemma; if Jesus tries to give a sign, he will fail; if he refuses, he will lose popular support. 'He sighed deeply' expresses deep emotion and indignation (see 3:5). It is a sigh in which both anger and sorrow have a part; obstinate sin stirred Jesus deeply.

As the generation which came up out of Egypt resisted Moses, so 'this generation' resisted Jesus. 'No sign will be given' – the Greek formula (*ei dothésetai*) is in fact a strong negation or an imprecation: 'May I die if God grants this generation a sign' (the passive points to God as agent). The refusal could not be more absolute. 'He left them' (v 13) because there was no scope for his ministry among them. He got into the boat again and crossed to 'the other side'; for Mark this is to Bethsaida (v 22), to the eastern shore of the lake. The crossing and recrossing of the lake, while hard to follow because of the imprecision of placenames, is certainly important for Mark as illustrating Jesus' bringing together of Jew and Gentile.

Jesus and the Disciples 8:14-21
The One Loaf

14Now the disciples had forgotten to bring any bread; and they had only one loaf with them in the boat. 15And he cautioned them, saying, 'Watch out – beware of the yeast of the Pharisees and the yeast of Herod.' 16They said to one another, 'It is because we have no bread.' 17And becoming aware of it, Jesus said to them, 'Why are you talking about having no bread? **Do you still not perceive or understand**? Are your hearts hardened? 18Do you have eyes, and fail to see? Do you have ears and fail to hear? And do you not remember? [19]When I broke the five loaves for the five thousand, how many baskets full of broken pieces did you collect?' They said to him, 'Twelve'. [20]And the seven for the four thousand, how many baskets full of broken pieces did you collect?' And they said to him, 'Seven.' [21]Then he said to them, '**Do you not yet understand**?'

Mark had, throughout, stressed the failure of the twelve to understand (4:13, 40-41; 6:52; 7:18; 8:4); in all cases they displayed lack of spiritual insight in failing to discern some hidden meaning in a word or deed of Jesus. The passage 8:14-21 is the climax of this theme in the first half of the gospel. A series of seven questions conveys Jesus' bitter disappointment at their tardiness. 'Do you not yet understand?' is the burden of this censure. Mark wrote with the special needs of his community in mind; therefore he has exaggerated the obtuseness of the disciples. The drama of the episode is present from the first: 'Now the disciples had forgotten to bring any bread; and they had only one loaf with them in the boat!' (v 41). The disciples, who had been actively involved in two miraculous feedings, where Jesus had satisfied the needs of great crowds, were now concerned because they were short of bread! They 'had only one loaf with them in the boat' – this is not just a vivid Marcan touch. The development of the passage will suggest that what the disciples failed to understand was that Jesus is the one loaf for Jews and Gentiles – as the feedings ought to have shown them (see 1 Cor 10: 16-17; 12:12-13).

Bracketed by the repeated, 'Do you not understand?' (vv 17, 21), the specific recalling of the two feedings is marked as the key factor of the passage. The unexpected emphasis – on the baskets of fragments – is a further indication that this is just where we must look. We are meant to see that the number (twelve) and the *cophinos*, a basket commonly used by Jews, point to the Jewish world, while the number seven (universal) and the ordinary basket (*spyris*) indicate the Gentile world. Those of Gentile background as well as those of Jewish origin are both at home in the household of the faith. And their fellowship is achieved in the breaking of the bread. The Christian who cannot or will not see this merits the charge: is your heart hardened? It would appear that Mark has some Jewish-Christian disciples primarily in view. The kind of situation that Paul encountered in Jerusalem and Antioch (Gal 2) would also have cropped up again at a later date in other areas. It would not have been easy for Pharisaic Jews, coming to Christianity, to shrug off their ingrained prejudice and enter into warm fellowship with Gentiles. Jesus, the 'one loaf', was the Messiah uniting Jew and Gentile about himself into one messianic people (see Eph 2:11-22).

Healing Of A Blind Man 8:22-26

22They came to Bethsaida. Some people brought a blind man to him and begged him to touch him. 23He took the blind man by the hand and led him out of the village; and when he had put saliva on his eyes and laid his hands on him, he asked him, 'Can you see any- thing?' 24And the man looked up and said, 'I can see people, but they look like trees, walking.' 25Then Jesus laid his hands on his eyes again; and he looked intently and his sight was restored, and he saw everything clearly. 26Then he sent him away to his home, saying, 'Do not even go into the village.'

This story rounds off the second 'loaves section' (8:1-26) just as the healing of the deaf-mute (7:31-37) had rounded off the first. Both stories are found only in Mark and the close parallelism between them has long been remarked. We have to do with a single scheme used for two different incidents, a scheme proper to these two accounts.

The situation of the story of the healing of the blind man (8:22-26) is calculated and its symbolic intent is manifest. It comes, dramatically, just after the castigation of the sheer hardness of heart, the total blindness, of the disciples (vv 14-21). It thereby symbolises the gradual opening of their eyes leading, at last, to a profession of faith (8:27-29). Indeed, the parallelism between vv 22-26 and 27-30 is remarkable. Jesus led the disciples away from the village(s), 27a (23a) and in two stages, at first imperfectly, 27b-28 (23-24), then fully, 29 (25), the truth about him was made plain. Jesus then imposed silence, 30 (26). The story is a sign of coming to faith. It tells us that Jesus alone could cure the blindness of the disciples, and it shows, too, that their lack of understanding was so serious that it could be penetrated only gradually. The second half of the gospel will show how imperfect that first glimmer of understand- ing was and how Jesus will have to struggle with their persistent obtuseness. The readers of the gospel are reminded that only the Lord can grant understanding.

Bethsaida was a town on the north shore of the lake, just east of the Jordan mouth. For Mark (6:45) this was 'the other side'. 'They brought to him ... and begged him to' (v 22) – verbally the same as 7:32. Again in v 23 there is much in common with 7:33 – the taking of the man aside, the use of spittle and the laying on of hands. 'Can you see anything?' – the question of Jesus in the course of working a miracle was unusual. This is the only cure in the gospels that is described as taking place gradually, in two stages. This factor may well have been a traditional device to bring out more graphically the difficulty of the healing and so add to the impressiveness of the miracle. But Mark saw it as an illustration of growth in faith (see vv 27-29). 'I can see people, but they look like trees, walking' (v 24) is a good rendering of an awkward Greek sentence. The idea is clear; the man was beginning to recover his sight, but as yet could not distinguish objects clearly. As in 7:35 the cure itself is vividly described in three co-ordinated phrases (v 25). 'Do not go into the village' (v 26); another, preferable, reading is; 'Do not tell anyone in the village.' This alternative reading would constitute a further link with the cure of the deaf mute: 'Then he ordered them to tell no one' (7:36).

There is another healing of a blind man, Bartimaeus, at 10:46-52. These two stories (8:22-26; 10:46-52) frame the intervening section. They stand, respectively, at the beginning and at the end of the way to Jerusalem and draw our attention to what Jesus had been doing: on the way he had striven to open the eyes of his disciples.

Mark has brought us to a turning-point of his gospel. He has striven to achieve the unity of his mixed community. It is the manifest will of the Lord that Gentiles should be called to salvation. Yet, the Lord, too, respected the divinely ordained division between the two peoples. Israel did have the right to hear the good news first. Still, the new way brought by Jesus is not a patching of the old nor a wine that can be poured into old wineskins. The new way of Jesus is just that: new. And in this age not only do rigid religious traditions have no place, but distinctions of clean and unclean have no meaning. Salvation is for all. Jesus is the one loaf for Jew and Gentile alike. Differences must be resolved in the unity of eucharistic fellowship. But the community still has much, everything indeed, to learn. Mark will teach them, in the words and example of Jesus, what it means to be a Christian.

You Are The Messiah 8:27-30

[27]Jesus went on with his disciples to the villages of **Caesarea Philippi**; and on the way he asked his disciples, 'Who do people say that I am?' [28]And they answered him, 'John the Baptist; and others, Elijah; and still others, one of the prophets.' [29]He asked them, 'But who do you say that I am?' Peter answered him, 'You are the Messiah.' [30]And he sternly ordered them not to tell anyone about him.

In the neighbourhood of Caesarea Philippi, on the slopes of Mount Hermon (v 27), Jesus and his disciples are 'on the way', ultimately, the way to Jerusalem, the way of the cross. His question prepares for the more personal and vital question of v 29. 'People', that is, those outside the circle of his disciples. For Mark, these 'outsiders' represent Israel. For a belief in a return of Elijah see Mal 3:1; 4:5. As Elijah was thought to have reappeared in John the Baptist, some felt that John had returned to life in his successor, Jesus. 'One of the prophets' reflects the expectation of 'the prophet like Moses' who was supposed to appear in the final days (see Jn 1:21). The obvious parallel between 8:28 and 6:14-16 is due to Mark who had perceived that the conjectures of the people and the superstitious fears of Herod (6:14-16) would serve to convey popular speculation about Jesus. He was regarded, at most, as a traditional forerunner of the Messiah.

'He asked them, "But who do you say that I am?" Peter answered him, "You are the Messiah".' (v 29). In the evangelist's eyes the unique significance of Peter's confession rests upon the fact that here, for the first time, the disciples told Jesus who, in their estimation, he was. Jesus took the initiative and put a direct question. Peter had at last begun to see: 'You are the Messiah.' The sequel will show that his understanding of Jesus' messiahship was quite wide of the mark.

Mark looked beyond Peter and the disciples to the community of his concern and bade his Christians take care that they really understood who their Christ is. There had been a studied preparation of the reader. From the start Mark had shown Jesus acting in an extraordinary manner which called forth the astonishment of the witnesses and led to a series of questions about him (1:27; 2:7; 6:2). Jesus himself heightened the effect (2:10, 28). Who is this Son of Man? Who is the Physician? (3:16-17). Who is this Bridegroom?

(2:19). The themes of the amazement of the crowd and the incomprehension of the disciples stand as a question-mark over the first eight chapters of the gospel. And now, for the Christians who read Mark, the confession, 'You are the Messiah' is their profession of faith. The warning is: that confession might be inadequate (8:32-33).

Conclusion and Transition 8:27-33

The central importance of Peter's confession in Mark's editorial structure is indicated by the brusque change of tone and of orientation after Peter has acknowledged the messiahship of Jesus. In the actual structure of the gospel the prediction of the passion (8:31-32a) is Jesus' response to the confession of Peter. The following section of the gospel (8:31–11:10) is dominated by the prophecies of the passion (8:31; 9:31; 10:33-34), each of which is placed in a different geographical locale: Caesarea Philippi (8:27), Galilee (9:30), and on the way to Jerusalem (10:32). The violent protestation of Peter in 8:32 shows clearly that this is a new and unexpected teaching. 'He said all this quite openly' – it is indeed a turning point in the self-revelation of Jesus: until now he had said nothing explicitly about his messiahship. If he still charges his disciples not to reveal his messianic identity (v 30) – because their understanding of him is still so imperfect – he now speaks to them quite plainly of his destiny of suffering and death. For, in Mark's intention, 8:31 becomes the starting-point of the way of Jesus which ends in Jerusalem with the women at the tomb.

'And Peter took him aside and began to rebuke him' (v 32b). The idea of a suffering Messiah was altogether foreign to Peter. Despite his confession he had not grasped the essential nature of messiahship. In his surprise and his upset at the unexpected prospect he dares to 'rebuke' Jesus. His acknowledgment of Jesus as Messiah had set him and the disciples apart from 'people' (v 27); but now Peter is rebuked for thinking as people think. Peter, and all like him who set their minds on 'human things', stand opposed to God's saving purpose and align themselves with Satan.

The passage, in truth, is less concerned with the historical situation of the mission of Jesus, than with the historical situation of the church for which Mark is writing. The reply to Jesus' first question refers to opinions available in the Palestinian situation of the ministry (v 28). But, in the reply to the second question, the title 'Messiah' (Christ) has Christian overtones, and the prediction of the passion is cast in language of the early church (vv 29, 31). Peter's reaction and the sharp correction of it (vv 32-33) have much to do with an understanding of christology. At the narrative level, Jesus and Peter engage in dialogue. At a deeper level, 'Jesus' is the Lord addressing his church and 'Peter' represents fallible believers who confess correctly, but then interpret their confession mistakenly. Similarly, the 'crowd' (v 34) is the people of God for whom the general teaching (8:34–9:1) is meant. Thus, a story about Jesus and his disciples has a further purpose in terms of the risen Lord and his church.

Here, more obviously than elsewhere, Mark is writing for his community. Here, above all, he is concerned with christology. The confession of Peter is the facile profession of too many of Mark's contemporaries: You are the Christ. Everything depends on what they mean by that profession and its influence on their lives. They cannot have a risen Lord without a suffering Messiah,. They cannot be his disciples without walking his road of suffering. Mark's admonition here is quite like that of Paul in Rom 8:15-17.

The specific details about place (v 27), and the designation of Peter as Satan (v 33), show that an historical nucleus lies within 8:27-33. But the end product is Marcan. On the basis of traditional data the evangelist has carefully composed the whole central part, the hinge of his gospel. And in it he has shown that the messianic story is no uninterrupted success story: it is a story of suffering, rejection, failure. This fact must influence and colour all we say about life and salvation. Jesus immediately runs into opposition: 'Peter … began to rebuke him.' Quite obviously, Peter has spoken for all of us. Jesus confirms this: 'You are setting your mind … on human things' – the natural reaction of those who shrink from a way of suffering. Have we, at bottom, any different idea of salvation from that of Peter? Can we really conceive of salvation other than in categories of victory? We experience the saying of Jesus again and again as contradiction, we cannot reconcile ourselves to it. The rebuke of Jesus did not change Peter: he will deny the suffering Messiah. The other disciples will sleep and will abandon him. And the church, which began with the twelve who failed to understand will, time and again, like them, fail to understand.

What is the meaning of the word that follows the prediction of suffering and death: ' … and after three days rise again'? These words are not meant to allay our fears, not meant to soften the stark reality of suffering and death. That word of victory of the Son of Man over death is a promise of victory for the oppressed, the vanquished, the silent in death – the forgotten. It is a word of warning against our human way of exalting the victorious and triumphant. Through the suffering Messiah victory is won by the vanquished; through the dead Messiah life is regained by the dead. He and his way are the sole guarantee of our victory and of our life.

A. The Way of the Son of Man 8:31–10:52

This, the first section of the second part of his gospel, is the unit in which Mark's *theologia crucis*, his central theological preoccupation, is most evident.

We can discern in it a precise pattern, signposted by three announcements of the fate of the Son of Man. Each time a passion prediction is followed by the theme of the incomprehension of the disciples. Then Jesus stresses the demands of discipleship – Mark makes the point that discipleship means following the Crucified one, that it is an *imitatio Christi*.

To imitate Christ is to follow his way; the phrase 'on the way' runs as a refrain through this section. At the outset, Jesus and his disciples are 'on the way' (8:27) and at the end, when they draw near to Jerusalem, Bartimaeus, restored to sight, followed Jesus 'on the way' (10:52). In between we are repeatedly reminded. 'On the way' the disciples had engaged in discussion on the issue of greatness (9:33-34). Jesus continued 'along the way' (10:17), and resolutely led the disciples 'on the way' to Jerusalem (10:52). The summons of 8:34 is given dramatic shape and content.

I. The First Prediction of the Passion and its Sequel 8:31–9:29

The Son of Man Must Suffer 8:31-33
[31]Then he began to teach them that the Son of Man must undergo great suffering, and be rejected by the elders, the chief priests, and the scribes, and be killed, and after three days rise again. [32]He said all this quite openly. And Peter took him aside and began to rebuke him. [33]But turning and looking at his disciples, he rebuked Peter and said, 'Get behind me, Satan! For you are setting your mind not on divine things but on human things.'

The prediction of the passion (v 31), closely attached to Peter's confession by the editorial injunction to silence (v 30) is, in some sort, the title of the second part of the gospel which begins at this point and will reach a climax on Calvary (15:39). 'Then he began to teach' – the words suggest a new orientation in the teaching of Jesus. Peter had just acknowledged Jesus to be the Messiah. Jesus employs the designation Son of Man to expound his understanding of what Messiah means (see 14:61-62). From now on the title will appear in connection with the passion and death of the Son of Man (9:9, 31; 10: 23, 45; 12: 31; 14:21) or with his glorious coming (8:38; 13:26; 14:62). 'Must' (*dei*) expresses a conviction that the sufferings of the Messiah are in accordance with the will of God revealed in scripture (see 9: 12). Luke (24:26-27) states clearly: 'Was it not necessary (*edei*) that the Messiah should suffer these things and then enter into his glory? ... He interpreted to them the things about himself in all the scriptures.' The passion of Jesus is not a quirk of fate.

 The opening words, 'The Son of Man must undergo great suffering' (see 9:12) give the prediction in its simplest form; the formulation of the rest of the verse has been coloured by the events, and the details have been conformed to the story of the passion. To this extent the prediction is a *vaticinium ex eventu*. 'Be rejected ... killed ... rise again' – an outline of the passion in its three stages: official rejection of the Messiah, his violent death, his vindication.

According to Mark, Jesus did refer to his death several times (see 8: 31; 9:9, 31; 10:34; 14:28), but surely in less explicit terms than these texts suggest.

'He said all this quite openly' (8:32) might be rendered: 'And openly he proclaimed the word.' This was the turning-point in the self-revelation of Jesus. If he still charged his disciples not to reveal his messianic identity (v 30), he now spoke to them quite openly of his messianic destiny of suffering and death. This emphatic affirmation that Jesus spoke openly (*parrésia*), see Jn 7:26; 10:24, of his passion shows the unusual character of the fact. Even when he had spoken 'privately' with his disciples he had never spoken so clearly. Here it is impossible to miss the meaning of his words, and Peter's reaction (v 32b) shows that he had at once understood what Jesus had said, even though the divine necessity for the suffering escaped him altogether.

'And Peter took him aside': we can picture him, in his earnestness, taking hold of Jesus, and 'rebuking' him. He seems, for the moment, to have forgotten who was Master and who disciple. The notion of a suffering Messiah was quite foreign to Peter. His confession, 'You are the Messiah,' turns out to have been a classic instance of 'verbal orthodoxy': the formula is correct; the understanding of it is quite mistaken. He realised, too, that his own situation would be affected; disciple of a suffering Messiah was not a role he relished. The phrase 'and he looked at his disciples' is proper to Mark: the rebuke is addressed to them also.

'Get behind me, Satan!' (*hypage opisó mou, Satana*) – the words recall Mt 4:10, 'Begone, Satan!' (*hypage, Satana*). This would suggest that Mark knew a form of the Matthew/Luke temptation story. The temptation in the wilderness (Mt 4:1-11; Lk 4:1-13) aimed at getting Jesus himself to conform to a popularly envisaged messianic role, to become a political messiah. It was an attempt to undermine his full acceptance of the will of God for him, and here Peter was playing Satan's role. Peter's acknowledgment of Jesus as Messiah had, in principle, set him apart from 'people' (v 27); but now he found himself rebuked for judging in an all too human manner. Peter, and all like him, who set their minds 'on human things' stand opposed to God's purpose and align themselves with Satan.

True Discipleship 8:34–9:1

8 [34]He called the crowd with his disciples, and said to them, 'If any want to become my followers, let them deny themselves and take up their cross and follow me. [35]For those who want to save their life will lose it, and those who lose their life for my sake, and for the sake of the gospel, will save it. [36]For what will it profit them to gain the whole world and forfeit their life? [37]Indeed, what can they give in return for their life? [38]Those who are ashamed of me and of my words in this adulterous and sinful generation, of them the Son of man will also be ashamed when he comes in the glory of the Father with the holy angels.'

9 [1]And he said to them, 'Truly I tell you, there are some standing here who will not taste death until they see that the kingdom of God has come with power.'

Coming directly after the first prediction of the passion (8:31-33), the passage 8:34–9:1 asserts, unequivocally, that the disciples of the Son of Man (v 31) must necessarily walk in his path. Jesus had 'called the crowd with his disciples' (v 34): this challenge was addressed to all. The loyal disciple would not be preoccupied with personal interests but would follow in sustained faithfulness to Jesus. The way of discipleship is not easy and one may be tempted to shrink from what it entails. To seek thus to evade risk and save one's life – to have things one's own way – would be to suffer the loss of one's true self. One prepared and willing to risk all for Jesus and for the good news is one who will achieve authentic selfhood. If human life on earth is so much more precious than anything else in creation, if no one can put a price on it, how much more precious the eternal life to be won by the faithful disciple. There is the challenge. A warning sounds for one who would not follow, for one who would draw back, ashamed of the Way, one who would seek to save one's life (see 4:14-19). Jesus, too, the warning rings, will be ashamed of such a one, will not acknowledge such a one, when he will reappear in glory at the end (v 38). But 'some standing here' will be witnesses of the vindication of the Son of Man ('after three days rise again', 8:31). Their witness sustains the faith of the Marcan community. Mark was still certain that a Christian had to come to terms with the cross. Once this had been grasped, one had to spread the good news (see 13:10)

Mark assuredly looked beyond the mission of Jesus. Like the author of Revelation, his concern was for the persecuted community of his day (see 13:9-13) – though, in neither case, was it yet all-out persecution. He reminded those followers of a rejected and crucified Messiah that it should not surprise that they, too, were called upon to suffer. The cross had turned the values of the world upside down – it is indeed a 'stumbling block' and 'foolishness' (see 1 Cor 1:23). They must be steadfast in face of persecution. They must not be ashamed of Jesus' way of humiliation and suffering and death, if they do not want the glorious Son of Man to be ashamed of them at his coming.

The Transfiguration. Listen to Him 9: 2-13

> [2]Six days later, Jesus took with him **Peter and James and John**, and led them up a high mountain apart, by themselves. And he was transfigured before them, [3]and his clothes became dazzling white, such as no one on earth could bleach them. [4]And there appeared to them Elijah with Moses, who were talking with Jesus. [5]Then Peter said to Jesus, 'Rabbi, it is good for us to be here; let us make three

dwellings, one for you, one for Moses, and one for Elijah.' [6]He did not know what to say, for they were terrified. [7]Then a cloud overshadowed them, and from the cloud there came a voice, 'This is my Son, the Beloved, listen to him!' [8]Suddenly when they looked around, they saw no one with them any more, but only Jesus.
[9]As they were coming down the mountain, he ordered them to tell no one about what they had seen, until after the Son of Man had risen from the dead. [10]So they kept the matter to themselves, questioning what this rising from the dead could mean. [11]Then they asked him, 'Why do the scribes say that Elijah must come first?' [12]He said to them, 'Elijah is indeed coming first to restore all things. How then is it written of the Son of Man, that he is to go through many sufferings and be treated with contempt? [13]But I tell you that Elijah has come, and they did to him whatever they pleased, as it is written about him.'

The transfiguration episode ranks with the baptism (1:9-11) and Gethsemane (14:32-42) narratives and shows similarities with both. While it is no longer possible to say what transpired upon the mountain – was it vision? Was it profound religious experience? – we must seek to understand what the episode meant for Mark. It certainly was important for him; this is signalled by the presence of the three privileged disciples. The transfiguration, involving a change in Jesus' form, would have been an anticipation of his glorified state.

In v 4 the order Elijah and Moses (Moses and Elijah is the traditional order) is unusual; it may simply be because Mark will go on to speak of the second Elijah (the Baptist, vv 11-13). 'Talking with Jesus' (v 4) – Luke gives the theme of the conversation: the 'departure' (literally, the exodus or death; see Wisdom 3:2; 7:6; 2 Peter 1:15) of Jesus at Jerusalem.

Luke's narrative (Lk 9:28-32) may be a pointer to the basic episode. In the entire first part of Luke's text Jesus held centre stage. He went up on a mountain, site of divine manifestation. He became absorbed in prayer and in the immediacy of communion with God his countenance was altered and his raiment shone with heavenly brightness. 'Two men' (Moses and Elijah) appeared to him and spoke with him of his 'departure'. Moses and Elijah stand for Law and prophets, the scripture of Israel. Later, the risen Lord will open the minds of the Emmaus disciples 'to understand the scriptures', that is, everything written about him in 'the law of Moses, the

THE WAY OF THE SON OF MAN

prophets and the psalms' (Lk 24:44-55). In other words, on the mountain, Jesus himself, through prayerful meditation on the scriptures, in an ineffable mystical experience, came to understand that his destiny was to suffer and to die.

In Mark, however, the aspect of revelation to Jesus yields wholly to the theme of revelation granted to the disciples. And now the entire first part of the narrative prepares for this. Jesus led the three disciples 'up a high mountain' where he was transfigured 'before them' (Mk 9:2). Elijah and Moses appeared 'to them' and it was for the disciples' benefit that a heavenly voice was heard, speaking of Jesus in the third person (9:7). 'It is good for us to be here' (v 5) – that is to say, this is a happy moment which ought to be prolonged indefinitely. Wholly forgotten is the word of the suffering and death of the Son of Man (8:31). Peter really 'did not know what to say'; he has, yet again, totally misunderstood. The voice from heaven sets the record straight 'This is my Son, the Beloved' – in contrast to 1:11 (the baptism), the words are here addressed to the disciples (instead of to Jesus): they hear the divine approbation of Jesus as the messianic Son. Suddenly, Elijah and Moses had disappeared and Jesus stood alone. 'Listen to him': the Beloved Son, whose love of Father and humankind will be proved in suffering and death, is the Revealer of the true God.

Mark intends us to see in the transfigured Jesus an anticipated glimpse of the risen Lord. As such, the episode is representative of that stage of christology which looked upon the resurrection as the decisive christological moment (see Rom 1:3-4; Acts 2:32-36; 5:30-31; 13:32-33). Because of his victory over death he has been designated Son of God in power. Three christological titles are brought close together: Messiah (8:29), Son of Man (8:31), Son of God (9:7). Jesus' divine sonship is the key to his status. All had become normal again (v 8). The disciples saw before them, quite alone, their Master, no longer transformed but in the familiar guise of every day.

The disciples had glimpsed the glory of Jesus; they would not understand 'until the Son of Man had risen from the dead' (9:9). Not until then could he be proclaimed with understanding and in truth. Typically, the disciples had not grasped the teaching, not even what 'resurrection' meant (v 10). Their problem was how could Jesus be raised from the dead before and apart from the gen-

eral resurrection at the end. It is a signal to the Christian; he or she
must strive to grasp the mighty, transforming import of the resurrection. It is a promise of life beyond the seeming finality of death.

The Elijah-passage (9:11-13) is an answer to a difficulty that faced
the early church. Christians believed that Jesus was the Messiah.
But Jewish tradition, based on Malachi 3:2-5; 4:5-6, held that Elijah's
return would precede 'the great and terrible day of the Lord'.
Implied in Mark's text (9:11) is a denial that Elijah had come. Jesus
answered that the tradition about Elijah was based on scripture.
The second part of the reply (vv 12b-13) faced up to another objection: the Christian claim that John the Baptist was the promised
Elijah-figure was disproved by the well-known fate of the Baptist.
The reply is in terms of Baptist-Jesus typology. The Baptist's fate
was prophetic of the fate of the Messiah. 'As it is written of him' –
see 1 Kings 19:2, 10 – John had found his Jezebel in Herodias (see
Mk 6:17-28). It was fitting that the precursor should, beforehand,
walk the way the Son of Man must walk – a point made explicitly in
Mt 17:12. The Christian retort to the Jewish objection was that John
was the perfect Elijah to the Messiah who would come.

An Epileptic Boy 9:14-29
   [14]When they came to the disciples, they saw a great crowd around
   them, and some scribes arguing with them. [15]When the whole
   crowd saw him, they were immediately overcome with awe, and
   they ran forward to greet him. [16]He asked them, 'What are you
   arguing about with them?' [17]Someone from the crowd answered
   him, 'Teacher, I brought you my son; he has a spirit that makes him
   unable to speak; [18]and whenever it seizes him, it dashes him down;
   and he foams and grinds his teeth and becomes rigid; and I asked
   your disciples to cast it out, but they could not do so.' [19]He
   answered them, 'You faithless generation, how much longer must I
   be among you? How much longer must I put up with you? Bring
   him to me.' [20]And they brought the boy to him. When the spirit saw
   him, immediately it convulsed the boy, and he fell on the ground
   and rolled about, foaming at the mouth. [21]Jesus asked the father,
   'How long has this been happening to him?' And he said, 'From
   childhood. [22]It has often cast him into the fire and into the water, to
   destroy him; but if you are able to do anything, have pity on us and
   help us.' [23]Jesus said to him, 'If you are able! – All things can be
   done for the one who believes.' [24]Immediately the father of the child
   cried out, 'I believe; help my unbelief!' [25]When Jesus saw that a
   crowd came running together, he rebuked the unclean spirit, saying

to it, 'You spirit that keeps the boy from speaking and hearing, I command you, come out of him, and never enter him again!' [26]After crying out and convulsing him terribly, it came out, and the boy was like a corpse, so that most of them said, 'He is dead.' [27]But Jesus took him by the hand and **lifted him up**, and he was **able to stand**. [28]When he had entered the house, his disciples asked him privately, 'Why could we not cast it out?' [29]He said to them, 'This kind can come out only through prayer.'

Mark has purposely placed the narrative of the epileptic demoniac directly after the transfiguration. As the heavenly acknowledgment of Jesus at the baptism (1:11) was followed by Satan's temptation (1: 12-13) so, too, the acknowledgment at the transfiguration (9:7) was followed by Jesus' encounter with a demon. The editorial verses 9: 14-16 are a bridge from the transfiguration to the healing of the epileptic. The central theme is the powerlessness of the disciples: Jesus was absent and nothing went right for them. They were unable to cope with an evil spirit and surely would have been out of their depth in theological debate with scribes (9:14-18).

In 9:18a the distressing symptoms of epilepsy are described (see v 20) – the recurrent convulsions and fits being ascribed to periodical assault by an evil spirit. 'They were not able' – Mark underlines the disciples' inability: not only the petitioner, but they themselves (v 28) were surprised to find that they were powerless. After all, they had been granted power over unclean spirits (6:7, 13); their former suc-cess (see 6:30) had gone to their heads. 'You faithless generation' (9:19) is an echo of Deut 32: 5 (see Mk 8:12). The reproof is general and expresses the weariness of Jesus in face of the lack of faith man-ifested by his contemporaries – in particular, the disciples.

Jesus' question, 'How long has this been happening to him?' (v 21a) serves to bring out the gravity of the malady (vv 21b-22). The seizure could have come upon the boy at any time, so he could have toppled into fire or water; the father attributed this to the malevo-lent spite of the evil spirit. 'But if you are able to do anything' – the man had been discouraged by the failure of the disciples. 'If you are able!' – Jesus fixed upon the lack of faith. 'All things can be done for one who believes'; not that faith can do everything, but that faith will set no limits to the power of God. 'I believe, help my unbelief!' (v 24) – the father admitted that his faith was defective. For its strengthening and growth it required the help of the Master – the

Christian overtones are obvious. With this cry from the heart the man emerged in a favourable light and stood in contrast to the disciples.

The baneful spirit was not only expelled but was bidden, 'never enter him again!' (v 25). Since the affliction was not continuous but recurrent the spirit must not only leave but must not return. 'Like a corpse' (v 26): the boy lay motionless and pallid; most of the crowd took him for dead. 'Took him by the hand' (see 1:31; 5:41), 'lifted him up' (see 1:31), 'he arose' (see 5:42) – the parallels with the healing of Peter's mother-in-law (1:29-31) and the raising of Jairus' daughter (5:35-43) are evident and deliberate. The theological language of the early church's preaching of the death and resurrection of Christ is even more marked in the present passage. The kerygmatic intent is more obvious, coming in the middle of a section dominated by predictions of the passion and resurrection (8:31-32; 9:30-32). The cure, worked by Jesus, was a symbol and a presage of resurrection from the dead. The theme comes dramatically here after the disciples' questioning about the meaning of rising from the dead (9:10).

In vv 28-29 Jesus was alone with the disciples 'in a house' and they questioned him 'privately' – the Greek phrase *kat' idian* being an unmistakable Marcan label. This esoteric message to the disciples is, in reality, addressed to the Christian community. Jesus explained why the disciples had been unable to cope with the unclean spirit: prayer was vitally necessary because the exorcist must rely wholly on the power of God. Some manuscripts add 'and fasting' (v 28). Its addition is understandable but wrongheaded – it misses the point of the story. Fasting would introduce something of one's own effort, whereas the point being precisely made is total reliance on the Lord.

This is the final exorcism story in Mark and the only one in the second part of the gospel. The motif of faith is firmly stressed. Jesus upraided the faithless generation: all – scribes and Pharisees, the people, the very disciples – have been without understanding and hardhearted. And the boy's father had doubted the power of Jesus: 'If you are able!' He was told that faith does not set limits to the power of God. His cry is the heart of the story; he acknowledged his lack of faith and looked to Jesus for help. At that moment he stood in sharp contrast to the Twelve who displayed their lack of trust. He is typically one of the ' little people' who believe. Jesus lifted up one who looked like a corpse, who was reckoned to be dead. Now the disciples learned what rising from the dead meant: Christ's victory over the forces of evil. Now they recognised the power and authority of Jesus. Only through union with their Lord in prayer will they share that same power. Bereft of his presence, stripped of communion with him, Christians are powerless and helpless.

II. The Second Prediction of the Passion and its Sequel 9:30–10:31

Prediction and Failure 9:30-34

[30]They went on from there and passed through Galilee. He did not want anyone to know it; [31]for he was teaching his disciples, saying to them, 'The Son of Man is to be **betrayed into human hands**, and they will kill him, and three days after being killed, he will rise again.' [32]But they did not understand what he was saying and were afraid to ask him. [33]Then they came to **Capernaum** and when he was in the house he asked them, 'What were you arguing about on the way?' [34]But they were silent, for on the way they had argued with one another who was the greatest.

The events of Caesarea Philippi and of the mount of transfiguration marked a new turn. Now the fateful journey to Jerusalem gets underway and, fittingly, the disciples are warned of the fate that awaits their Master. It is a revelation granted to them alone, but they do not understand and are afraid. This second time Jesus' passion and resurrection are proclaimed in Galilee and in the context of a journey. In 9:9 we were shown that the need for secrecy about Jesus as Son of God was connected with the passion and resurrection of Jesus as Son of Man. Now the very person of Jesus is shrouded in secrecy as he teaches his disciples about that mystery of death and life.

The kernel of the second prediction – 'The Son of man is to be betrayed [delivered up] into human hands' – is likely to be close to the form of the earliest passion-saying which underlay the developed versions of the three predictions. In Aramaic it would run something like: 'God will (soon) deliver up the son of man to the sons of men.'

'Betrayed' (v 31): the verb *paradidómi* is notable in the second half of the gospel. Its meaning is 'deliver up', 'betray,' 'arrest.' It occurs twice in the first half. It is a highly significant term, with overtones of a divine purpose.

The key to it is in Acts 2:23. Peter is addressing the Jews: 'This Jesus delivered up (*exdidómi*) according to the definite plan and fore-knowledge of God, you crucified and killed by the hands of lawless men.' This does not mean some cold, inflexible plan. It is rather a way of insisting that, strange though it may seem, there is a divine purpose to this tragic drama. A list of the occurrences of the verb will illustrate how pervasive it is:

Paradidómi – 'deliver up'; ' betray'

1:14 After John was arrested [delivered up].
3:19 And Judas Iscariot, who betrayed him [delivered him up].
9:31 The Son of Man will be delivered into the hands of men.
10: 33 The Son of Man will be delivered to the chief priests.
13:9 They will deliver you up.
13:11 When they bring you to trial and deliver you up.
13:12 Brother will deliver up brother to death.
14:10 Judas Iscariot went to the chief priests in order to betray him [deliver him up] to them.
14:11 He sought an opportunity to betray him [deliver him up].
14:18 One of you will betray me [deliver me up].
14:21 Woe to that man by whom the Son of man is betrayed [delivered up].
14:41 The Son of man is betrayed [delivered up] into the hands of sinners.
14:44 Now the betrayer [deliverer up] had given them a sign.
14:42 See, my betrayer [the one who will deliver me up] is at hand.
15: 1 And delivered him to Pilate.
15:10 He perceived that it was out of envy that the chief priests had delivered him up.
15:15 Having scourged Jesus, he delivered him up to be crucified

The disciples had been bewildered by Jesus' further reference to his suffering (v 32). Now (v 34) their profound lack of understanding appears at its most blatant. They, disciples of a Master so soon to suffer bitter humiliation and death – they are 'on the way' to the

Jerusalem where it will take place – are all too humanly involved in petty squabbling over precedence.

Jesus Instructs the Disciples 9:35-50

[35]He sat down, called the twelve, and said to them, 'Whoever wants to be first must be last of all and servant of all.' [36]Then he took a little child and put it among them; and taking it in his arms, he said to them, [37]'Whoever welcomes one such child in my name welcomes me, and whoever welcomes me welcomes not me but the one who sent me.'

[38]John said to him, 'Teacher, we saw someone casting out demons in your name, and we tried to stop him, because he was not following us. [39]But Jesus said, 'Do not stop him; for no one who does a deed of power in my name will be able soon afterward to speak evil of me. [40]Whoever is not against us is for us. [41]For truly I tell you, whoever gives you a cup of water to drink because you bear the name of Christ will by no means lose the reward.'

[42]If any of you put a stumbling block before one of these little ones who believe in me, it would be better for you if a great millstone were hung around your neck and you were thrown into the sea. [43]If your hand causes you to stumble, cut it off; it is better for you to enter life maimed than to have two hands and go to hell, to the unquenchable fire. [45]And if your foot causes you to stumble, cut it off; it is better for you to enter life lame than to have two feet and to be thrown into hell. [47]And if your eye causes you to stumble, tear it out; it is better for you to enter the kingdom of God with one eye than to have two eyes and to be thrown into hell, [48]where their worm never dies, and the fire is never quenched.'

[49]'For everyone will be salted with fire. Salt is good; but if the salt has lost its saltiness, how can you season it? Have salt in yourselves, and be at peace with one another.'

Jesus took his seat and called the Twelve to him. 'Taking it in his arms' (see 10:16) – proper to Mark; a vivid touch in his style. The taking of the child is a symbolic action in the manner of the prophets. 'Receives' means the loving service of the weaker members of the community, those who stand in greatest need of being served. 'In my name,' that is, because of one's connection with me, because one belongs to me. A Christian is one baptised 'into the name of' Jesus (Mt 28:19; 1 Cor 1:13, 15), so becoming his. That is why one meets (serves) Christ himself in the disciple, and the Father in Christ. This, then, is the dignity of Christian service.

Francis Moloney has perceptively pointed to a feature of childhood that is immediately relevant here:

Jesus places a child in the midst of the disciples. The child becomes the focus of attention as the disciples are asked to stop looking at themselves. Perhaps offering a glimmer of his own personality, Jesus takes the child in his arms. But the message to the disciples, not Jesus' personality, is the point of the narrative. It is the child, held in the arms of Jesus, who best typifies what it is like to be 'with him' (see 3:14), something that is becoming increasingly difficult for the disciples. The teaching of Jesus that flows from the gesture further explains what it means to be last of all and servant of all (v 35). The universal experience of a young child, eyes open and questions flowing, is the reception of as much as possible from the new and exciting world he or she is beginning to experience. The feature highlighted by Jesus' words to the disciples is 'receptivity'. The verb *dechomai*, 'to receive,' is found four times in 9:37. There is an intimate link between 'receiving' the child, 'receiving' Jesus, and 'receiving' the one who sent Jesus. The service of the disciple will be found in service of those who look to them for such service. The child is not a 'prop' for Jesus' teaching. The child refers to others who believe in Jesus, but who still have much to learn. They must be 'received' as Jesus received the child, and this theme will return in 9:42-50. But the disciple is also called to 'receive' Jesus, and thus the one who sends him. When the disciples asked why they failed to drive out the evil spirit from the possessed boy (vv 14-19), Jesus spoke of the need for prayer (vv 28-29). Disciples are called to be receptive to one another, and also to the design of God, to be found in prayer. They are called to service in the believing community, but also to a profound receptivity to all that Jesus asks of them, and that includes the cross (see 9:30-31), rather than the glory expected by those considered the 'greatest' among them (see v 34). (*The Gospel of Mark*, 188-189).

Mark has made the point that the revelation of Jesus cannot be received by one who is not ready to enter into the spirit of discipleship and thereby become 'last' and 'servant'. As it stands, the passage is a pronouncement story: the point of it lies in the sayings of vv 35b and 37 (with the symbolic gesture of v 36 underlining the message). Jesus acknowledges that there is greatness in discipleship: the dignity, the greatness, of service. And this is so because the

loving service of the least member of the community is service of
Jesus and of the Father. At the start (v 33) Mark had drawn the special attention of his readers to this teaching, and to all that will be
said until v 50. Perhaps the reader of today is once again attuned to
the unambiguous message of this word of Jesus: greatness in his
church is found in *diakonia*, service, and only there. Our first step is
to have relearned this. It is high time for us to act accordingly, at all
times, and at all levels.

The outside exorcist 9:38-40

The practice of exorcism was widespread in the Hellenistic period
among both Jews and Gentiles. See Acts 19:13-16. The episode of an
exorcist who was not a disciple is linked to the preceding passage
by the catchword 'in my name', here meaning an exorcism worked
by invocation of the name of Jesus. The exorcist was 'not following
us', that is, not a disciple. Not following *us*: the disciples have
become arrogant. The fact of casting out demons 'in the name of
Jesus' shows that the exorcist acknowledged the authority of Jesus;
he was not opposed to Jesus and his disciples even if he was not
part of them. The saying of Jesus – 'No one who does a deed of
power in my name will be able soon afterward to speak evil of me'
(v 39) – offered his disciples a directive: they were not to forbid one
who acts so. In the context it is a matter of successful exorcism: the
person was 'casting out demons' (v 38) and Jesus spoke of a 'mighty
work' done by invocation of his name. The presumption is that one
who performs a good deed in the name of Jesus cannot be an enemy
of his. The saying of v 40 – 'Whoever is not against us is for us' –
suits the context perfectly. In a Christian setting, the statement
means that one belongs in Jesus' church as long as one does not cat-
egorically separate oneself from him.

Scandal 9:42-50

Jesus had come to seek out and save the lost. He came preaching
good news to the poor: to all the needy, helpless, defenceless ones.
Now he utters a grim warning against any who would hurt these
'little ones who believe in me', the humblest members of the
Christian community. Any who would shake their faith in him
would snatch from them the hope that he has given them. The
warning is very sharp. But one's own enemy, one's stumbling
block, may be within oneself (see 7:20-23). With the compelling

emphasis of startling metaphor and threefold repetition (vv 43, 45, 47) the Lord urges people to make the costliest sacrifices in order to avoid sin and enter into life. The language is the exuberant language of Semitic rhetoric. Only crass literalism could have led to the later notion of hell as a place of fiery torment. One should recall the earlier assurance: 'Truly, I tell you, people will be forgiven for their sins [God will forgive] and whatever blasphemies they utter' (3:28). God is ever God of forgiveness.

In the obscure word on 'salt' (v 50) Mark seems to refer to the spirit of discipleship. 'Salt' is a quality of the disciple. Christ's followers are meant to a purifying and seasoning element in the world. If they fail they cannot draw power from the world to which they are sent and which they serve. The saying of v 50b might be understood in the sense of Col 4:6 – 'Let your speech always be gracious, seasoned with salt.' Salt symbolises wisdom which ought to 'season' the words we speak to one another and so maintain peace in the Christian community. In its present context the saying would seem to say more than that. The meaning probably is: 'Have salt in yourselves, then you will be at peace with yourselves.' 'Be at peace with one another' – this constitutes a characteristic inclusion: the occasion of the discourse was a quarrel among the disciples (9:33-34); it is terminated by a recommendation to live at peace with one another. (see 1 Thess 5:13).

What God has joined together 10:1-12

1He left that place and went to the region of Judea and beyond the Jordan. And crowds again gathered around him; and, as was his custom, he again taught them.

2Some Pharisees came, and to test him they asked, 'Is it lawful for a man to divorce his wife? 3He answered them, 'What did Moses command you?' 4They said, 'Moses allowed a man to write a certificate of dismissal and to divorce her.' 5But Jesus said to them, 'Because of your hardness of heart he wrote this commandment for you. 6But from the beginning of creation, God made them male and female.' 7For this reason a man shall leave his father and mother and be joined to his wife, and the two shall become one flesh. So they are no longer two, but one flesh. 9Therefore what God has joined together, let no one separate.'

10Then in the house the disciples asked him about this matter. 11He said to them, 'Whoever divorces his wife and marries another commits adultery against her; 12and if she divorces her husband and marries another, she commits adultery.'

Jesus is on the way to Jerusalem (see 10:32). He moved 'beyond the Jordan', that is to say, to Peraea, a territory on the opposite side of the Jordan from Judaea; with Galilee, it formed the domain of Herod Antipas. Crowds flocked to him again and he resumed his teaching activity – Mark emphasises this by his repetition of 'again'. Jesus had invited his disciples to take up the cross (8:31–9:1) and to service and receptivity (9:35-50). Now he turns from theory to prac- tice – in the areas of marriage (10:2-12) and wealth (10:17-27). In vv 2-10 Jesus argues with Pharisees in rabbinical style. Question (v 2) is matched by counter-question (v 3). Nowhere in the written Torah is there legislation for divorce as such. The precise provision of Deut 24:1-4 shows divorce to be a custom taken for granted, the right of a husband to repudiate his wife without her having any redress. Jesus (v 5) does not contest his Pharisee questioner's interpretation of the law. He does declare that Moses had written the 'command- ment' on divorce because of human *sklérocardia*, 'hardness of heart', our unteachableness, our failure to acknowledge God's moral demands and to obey the higher principle proposed in Genesis. Jesus pressed the argument further by asserting that, from the beginning, God had no divorce in mind. By creating male and female God intended marriage to be for one man and one woman bound together in the indissoluble union implied by 'one flesh' (Gen 1:27; 2:24). This monogamous union, moreover, was indeed unbreakable not only by reason of the two being one, but also because God brings the partners together and is author of the mar- riage union: 'Therefore what God has joined together, let no man separate' (v 9). In the fashion of rabbinical debate, the Pharisees are reduced to silence.

An appendix (vv 10-12) to the pronouncement story is presented as an exposition which Jesus gave his disciples in private – the Marcan device which serves to adapt and broaden a teaching of Jesus. Verse 11 declares that not only is divorce forbidden but also that marriage following divorce constitutes adultery because the first marriage bond had not been severed. The words, 'against her', referring to a man's first wife, go beyond Jewish law which does not consider that a man commit adultery against his own wife (adultery was infringement of the right, the property indeed, of a husband; it was offence against the injured husband). The statement of v 12 goes quite beyond Jewish law where a woman was not permitted to divorce her husband. Mark has expanded the teaching of Jesus to meet the situation of Gentile Christians living under Graeco-Roman law. Moreover, there is the implication of equality and mutual responsibility within marriage. That responsibility can be costly.

It is essential to recognise that Jesus made his pronouncement on divorce on the assumption that the marriage was a true marriage. Not only had he stressed the interpersonal relationship of husband and wife, he had, by his prohibition of divorce, struck a blow for the equality of women. Furthermore, in any discussion of the New Testament's position on divorce, one must give due weight to Paul's stance in 1 Cor 7:10-16. He was fully aware of Jesus' teaching: 'To the married I give this command – not I but the Lord – that the wife should not be separated from her husband' (v 10). Nevertheless, he could still advocate divorce: 'If the unbelieving partner separates, let it be so; in such a case the brother or sister is not bound' (v 15). The case at issue is the marriage of a Christian and a pagan where the non-Christian spouse does not want the marriage to continue. The significant factor is that Paul, obviously, did not regard the prohibition of divorce as inflexible divine law. This is just how the Latin church has come to regard it. But, is this really what Jesus had meant? Rightly understood, his shift from what Moses wrote (Mark 10:3-4) to what God had intended (vv 6-7) – a shift from divorce to marriage – lifted the discussion out of the realm of legalism and set it in the realm of gift and grace.

The question surely must be asked whether the perception of divorce exclusively in terms of law may not account for a messy pastoral situation that cannot really be squared with the attitude and praxis of Jesus. Why is it that only in the situation of marital failure does the church seem unable to offer compassionate and effective help and healing – as it is quite able to do in all other forms of human failure and sin? Pastoral practice would be different if it were seen that Jesus had proposed an ideal, one to be urged and courageously supported, but which did not paint us into a corner. And, to be honest, pastoral practice does, often enough, depart from the official line. It does when a pastor dares to ask the question: What would Jesus do?

Let the Children come to me 10:13-16

> [13]People were bringing little children to him in order that he might touch them; and the disciples spoke sternly to them. [14]But when Jesus saw this, he was indignant and said to them, 'Let the little children come to me; do not stop them; for it is to such as these that the kingdom of God belongs. [15]Truly I tell you, whoever does not receive the kingdom of God as a little child will never enter it.' [16]And he took them up in his arms, laid his hands on them, and blessed them.

The passage 10:13-16 is a pronouncement story showing Jesus' attitude to children; its place here is on topical grounds, due, very likely, to the preceding teaching on marriage. Mark has delightfully brought the little scene to life: mothers anxious to present their children to the renowned Rabbi and wonder-worker; the disciples officiously intervening; Jesus indignant at their rebuff to children; his taking them into his arms (see 9:36).

The point of the narrative lies in the sayings. The disposition of a child – receptivity, a willingness to accept what is freely given – is necessary for all who would enter the kingdom. Children, better than any other, are suited for the kingdom since the kingdom is a gift which must be received with simplicity. Jesus himself, in a true sense, is the kingdom; that is why children have a right of access to him. The solemn 'Amen' (Truly I tell you) confirms the seriousness of the pronouncement of v 15. One must receive the kingdom as a child receives it, with trustful simplicity and without laying any claim to it. Here the kingdom is presented both as a gift which people receive and a sphere into which they enter: one must be willing to receive the kingdom as gift before one can enter into the blessings and responsibilities of it.

Possessions and Discipleship 10:17-31

> [17]As he was setting out on a journey, a man ran up and knelt before him, and asked him, 'Good Teacher, what must I do to inherit eternal life?'
> [18]Jesus said to him, 'Why do you call me good? No one is good but God alone. [19]You know the commandments: You shall not murder; You shall not commit adultery; You shall not steal; You shall not bear false witness; You shall not defraud; Honour your father and mother.' He said to him, 'Teacher, I have kept all these since my youth.' [21]Jesus, looking at him, loved him, and said, 'You lack one thing; go, sell what you own, and give the money to the poor, and

you will have treasure in heaven; then come, follow me.' 22When he heard this, he was shocked and went away grieving, for he had many possessions.

23Then Jesus looked around and said to his disciples, '**How hard** it will be for those who have wealth **to enter the kingdom of God!**' 24And the disciples were perplexed at these words. But Jesus said to them again, 'Children, **how hard it is to enter the kingdom of God**! 25It is easier for a camel to go through the eye of a needle than for someone who is rich to enter the kingdom of God.' 26They were greatly astounded and said to one another, 'Then who can be saved?' 27Jesus looked at them and said, 'For mortals it is impossible, but not for God; for God all things are possible.

28Peter began to say to him, 'Look, we have left everything and followed you.' 29Jesus said, 'Truly I tell you, there is no one who has left house or brothers or sisters or mother or father or children or fields, for my sake and for the sake of the good news, 30who will not receive a hundredfold now in this age – houses, brothers and sisters, mothers and children, and fields, with persecution – and in the age to come, eternal life. 31But many who are first will be last, and the last will be first.'

Jesus' teaching on the hazard of riches (10:23-27) and on the reward of renunciation (vv 28-31) was provoked by the incident of vv 17-22. This is the saddest story in the gospel, this story of the refusal of one whom Jesus loved to answer his call. Entry into the kingdom is the matter and issue as Jesus was asked what one must do to inherit eternal life. He began to answer the question by pointing to the duties towards one's neighbour prescribed in the decalogue; but he knew that observance of the law was not the whole answer. He was drawn to the man and invited him to become his disciple. This aspiring disciple had to learn that discipleship is costly: he, a wealthy man, was asked to surrender the former basis of his security and find his security in Jesus' word. He failed to see that following Jesus was the true treasure, the one pearl of great price (Mt 13:44, 46) beyond all his possessions. He could not face the stern challenge of loving in deed and in truth by opening his heart to his brother or sister in need (see 1 Jn 3:17-18). He was not receptive.

The rich man's sad departure (Mk 10:22) was dramatic evidence that riches could come between a person and the following of Jesus; the words of Jesus (vv 23-27) drove the message home. Jesus began by stressing the difficulty, for the wealthy, of access to the kingdom (v 23) and passed quickly to the difficulty of entering the kingdom at all (v 24). A vivid example of the impossible – 'It is easier for a camel to go through the eye of a needle than for someone who is rich to enter the kingdom of God' (v 25) (contrast of the largest beast known in Palestine with the smallest domestic aperture) – applied as it is to the rich, would come more logically before v 24. The point is that salvation is ever God's achievement, never that of humans (v 27) It is the only answer, the confident answer, to the helpless question, 'Then who can be saved?' (v 26). Seemingly complex, a paraphrase of 10:23-26 shows that the thought is not difficult to follow: How hard indeed it is for anyone to enter the kingdom, but for rich people it is quite impossible. In fact, humanly speaking, it is impossible for anyone to be saved, rich or not; but with God all things are possible. This is Paul's teaching in Romans.

All attempts to soften the hard saying of Jesus (v 25) contradict Mark's obvious intent. The concern throughout vv 17-31 was the problem of wealth in relation to the kingdom of God. The fact that the disciples were reported as being 'perplexed' (v 26) and 'astounded' (v 26) at Jesus' words, together with their question with regard to who can be saved (v 26), suggests that they believed the prosperity of the rich to be a sign of God's blessing. Mark, however, has presented wealth as a stumbling block or insurmountable barrier on the way to the kingdom. Can the rich be saved? Jesus acknowledged that salvation for the rich was possible, but it was possible only through the power of God (v 27). The point of this saying is that God will have to work a miracle of conversion in the hearts of the rich in order for them to be saved. It is so hard for those with wealth to divest themselves of their material possessions, and the security and power that seem to come with them, that it will take divine intervention to free the rich from their bondage.

The passage that follows (10:28-31) directs the reader's attention to a group of individuals, Peter and the disciples, who have overcome the lure of possessions and left their families, homes and occupations to follow Jesus in a life of discipleship. This does not mean, however, that to be a disciple one must be destitute. Jesus promised that those who forsake all for the kingdom will receive a hundredfold in this life. Despite his pattern as itinerant prophet and teacher, Jesus was no ascetic. The life of the poor, with its hardship and suffering, is not set forth in Mark's gospel as an ideal for the Christian

disciple. But, neither is the desire for possessions nor the accumul-
ation of wealth a reflection of the will of God.

The disciples had left all; Peter stated the fact with some complacency (v 28). His implicit question is made explicit in Mt 19:27 –
'What then will we have?' The items listed (v 29), given disjunctively,
included all possessions under the heads of home, relatives and
property. Significant is an omission in v 30. Verse 29 runs: 'No one
who has left house or brothers or sisters or mother or father or
children or fields,' while v 30 runs: 'houses, brothers and sisters,
mothers and children, and fields – 'fathers' are absent! This is a factor in the growing evidence that Jesus had envisaged a discipleship
of equals. He surely did not have in mind (given his distinctive
view of authority) a patriarchal model, with its pattern of domination. 'With persecutions' (v 30) – this may be meant to give an iron-
ical twist to the hundredfold 'reward' for total renunciation. More
simply, it reflects the harsh reality of Christian experience. Yet,
despite the afflictions which assailed them, early Christians found
abundant compensation in their new brotherhood and sisterhood
(see Rom 16:13). The saying of v 31 occurs also, in a wholly different
context, in Mt 20:16; Lk 13:30. We have no way of knowing, with
certainty, the original import of the saying. Mark, seemingly,
understands it to mean that while the rich and prosperous are first
in this world, those who have left all things (and consequently are
last here below) will be first in the world to come.

The Third Prediction of the Passion and its Sequel 10:32-45

[32]They were on the road, going up to Jerusalem, and Jesus was
walking ahead of them; they were amazed and those who followed
were afraid. He took the twelve aside again and began to tell them
what was to happen to him, [33]saying, 'See, we are going up to
Jerusalem, and the Son of Man will be **handed over** to the chief
priests and the scribes, and they will condemn him to death; then
they will hand him over to the Gentiles; [34]they will mock him, and
spit upon him, and flog him, and kill him; and after three days he
will rise again.'
[35]James and John, the sons of Zebedee, came forward to him and
said to him, 'Teacher, we want you to do for us whatever we ask of
you.' [36]And he said to them, 'What is it you want me to do for you?'
[37]And they said to him, 'Grant us to sit, one at your right hand and
one at your left, in your glory.' [38]But Jesus said to them, 'You do not

know what you are asking. Are you able to drink the cup that I drink, or be baptised with the baptism that I am baptised with?' [39]They replied, 'We are able.' Then Jesus said to them, 'The cup that I drink you will drink; and with the baptism with which I am baptised you will be baptised; [40]but to sit at my right hand or at my left is not mine to grant, but it is for those for whom it has been prepared.'

[41]When the ten heard this, they began to be angry with James and John. [42]So Jesus called them and said to them, 'You know that among the Gentiles those whom they recognise as their rulers lord it over them, and their great ones are tyrants over them. **[43]But it is not so among you**; but whoever wishes to be great among you must be your servant; [44]and whoever wishes to be first among you must be slave of all. [45]For the Son of Man came not to be served but to serve, and to give his life a ransom for many.'

The third and lengthiest prediction of the passion (10:33-34) corresponds very closely with the stages of the passion narrative in chapter 15. Mark had already presented Jerusalem as the centre of hostility to Jesus. Twice he has mentioned that hostile scribes, come from Jerusalem, had engaged in controversy with him (3:22; 7:10). This present journey is headed for a clash in Jerusalem with 'the chief priests, the scribes, and the elders' (11:27-33). 'Jesus was walking ahead of them' (10: 32) – he knew where he was going and what fate awaited him in the city. Luke (9:51) has put it aptly: 'When the days drew near for him to be taken up, he set his face to go to Jerusalem.' The resolute bearing of Jesus as he led the way stirred the disciples with amazement and a sense of foreboding – but they still followed him. As for Jesus himself, perhaps, again, Luke has put his finger on Mark's intent: 'I must be on my way, because it is impossible for a prophet to be killed outside of Jerusalem' (Lk 13:33). After this, Mark's Gethsemane scene (Mk 14:32-42) will come as a surprise. It will come as comfort for all who strive to 'follow' Jesus (see 8:34).

It is not so among you 10:35-45

Sadly, the stark words of vv 33-34 fell on ears deafened by selfish ambition (vv 35-37). Jesus had asked of one who would follow him a readiness to face and share his sufferings. Now the request of the brothers James and John is naïvely direct: the first places in Jesus' messianic kingdom no less! When Jesus asked them whether they had considered the price to be paid for a share in his glory they responded with brash confidence (v 39). 'The cup that I drink' – in the Old Testament 'cup' is a symbol both of joy and of suffering; our context demands the latter sense and, specifically, the idea of redemptive messianic suffering (see Mk 8:31; 9:31; 14:36; Jn 18:11). 'The baptism that I am baptised with': the 'baptism' is the passion which will 'plunge' Jesus into a sea of suffering. The brothers are being told: you do not know the price that must be paid to share my glory. Here indeed it is like Master like servant – and Jesus must suffer these things before entering into his glory (Lk 24:26). They must be prepared to accept the full implication of following Jesus. The power of the risen Lord would in due course break through the self-interest of James and John and give backbone to their facile enthusiasm; they will indeed courageously walk in the way of their master. We may well find something of ourselves in this pair.

The other ten were no less uncomprehending than James and John; they were indignant at being circumvented by the shrewd twins (v 41). This was an appropriate occasion for another lesson in disciple-ship(vv 42-45). Jesus solemnly asserted that, in the community of his disciples, there is no place for ambition. His church is a human society; there is place for authority, for leaders. But those who lead will serve their brothers and sisters: the spirit of authority is *diakonia* (service). Surely Jesus had intended the paradox and had asked for it to be taken seriously. He first outlined the accepted standard of civil authority: domination, with leaders lording it over their sub-jects, making their presence felt in all areas of life (10:42). Then (v 43) he asserted that this was not, positively not, to be the pattern for those who professed to follow him. Jesus stood authority on its head. Greatness would be measured by service: the leader will be slave (*doulos*) of the community. There could be no place at all for styles and trappings and exercise of authority after the model of civil powers and princes. Is there anything in the gospels quite as categorical as this demand?

The ground of the paradoxical behaviour required of disciples is to be found in the example of the Son of Man (v 45). Here this distinc-tive authority (*exousia*) with its firm stamp of *diakonia* (service) is given christological underpinning. The saying – 'For the Son of Man came not to be served but to serve, and to give his life a ransom for many [all]' – specifies in what sense Jesus would 'serve' people: he would give his life for them. *Lytron* ('ransom') was originally a commercial term; the ransom is the price that must be paid to redeem a pledge, to recover a pawned object, or to free a slave. In the Septuagint the term is predicated metaphorically of God who is frequently said to have bought, acquired, ransomed his people (e.g. Ps 49:8; Is 63:4). In its Marcan form the saying is related to Is 53:10-11 and 'ransom' is to be understood in the sense of the Hebrew word *asham* of Is 53:10, an 'offering for sin', an atonement offering. By laying down his life for a humankind enslaved to sin, Jesus fulfilled the word about the Servant in Is 53:10-11. Jesus had paid the universal debt; he gave his life to redeem all others. But this is metaphor, not crude commerce. The death of Jesus, in the Father's purpose and in the Son's acceptance, was a gesture of sheer love: 'Surely, they will respect my Son ... not what I want, but what you want' (Mk 12:6; 14:36). Any suggestion that the death of the Son was the literal payment of a debt, the placating of an offended God, is blasphemy – though it has been a tragic misperception of Christians. God is ever motivated by love, not 'justice'.

This word of Jesus was clear. Would it be heard? Not throughout Christian history. But it was heard in the Jerusalem of Jesus' day, and heard by the Roman power, heard as subversive of authority. Jesus was dangerous and had to be silenced. His teaching was political dynamite.

He Followed Him on the Way 10:46–52

46They came to Jericho. As he and his disciples and a large crowd were leaving Jericho, Bartimaeus, son of Timaeus, a blind beggar, was sitting by the roadside. 47When he heard that it was Jesus of Nazareth, he began to shout out and say, 'Jesus, Son of David, have mercy on me!' 48Many sternly ordered him to be quiet, but he cried out even more loudly, 'Son of David, have mercy on me!' 49Jesus stood still and said, 'Call him here.' And they called the blind man, saying to him, 'Take heart; get up, he is calling you.' 50So throwing off his cloak, he sprang up and came to Jesus. 51Then Jesus said to him, 'What do you want me to do for you?' The blind man said to him, 'My teacher, let me see again.' 52Jesus said to him, 'Go; **your faith has made you well.**' Immediately he regained his sight and **followed him on the way**.

Jesus and his disciples are now (v 46) well on the road to Jerusalem (v 32); Jericho is situated only fifteen miles north east of the city. 'A large crowd' – a concourse of pilgrims on the way to the holy city for Passover. A blind beggar was not an unusual sight; his position

outside the town gate on the road to Jerusalem was an advanta-
geous pitch. This narrative focuses on the blind man, who is presented as a model of faith in Jesus in spite of discouragement, and
as one who eagerly answered the call of the Master and followed
him in the way of discipleship. The story is as much a call story as a
healing story. For Mark the story sounds a new departure in the
self-manifestation of Jesus. He heard himself acclaimed, repeatedly,
as 'Son of David', a messianic title. Far from imposing silence, as
hitherto, he called the man to his presence and openly restored his
sight. The days were near for him to be delivered up and he had set
his face to go to Jerusalem (10:32; see Lk 9:51). Very soon the true
nature of his messiahship would be clearly seen.

We have observed that the story of the healing of a blind man in 8:
22-26 has a manifestly symbolical meaning in reference to the opening of the disciples' eyes. We can assume that Mark has a purpose
in placing a healing miracle at this point too. These two stories (8:
22-26; 10:46-52) frame the intervening section. They stand, respectively, at the beginning and at the end of the way to Jerusalem and
draw our attention to what Jesus had been doing: on the way he
had striven to open the eyes of his disciples.

Like the blind man in John 9, Bartimaeus emerges as a forthright
and attractive character. Jesus asked the man, 'What do you want
me to do for you?' The question is the same as that, shortly before (v
36) to the brothers James and John in response to their request. The
simple and humble request of Bartimaeus, 'Rabbouni, let me see
again' was so different from their arrogant demand; he understood
so much better than they the authority of a Jesus who had come to
serve. Unlike them (v 39) he was aware of his need and his helpless-
ness and found his only hope in Jesus' nearness. And Jesus
responded to his need: 'Your faith has made you well' (v 52). At a
deeper level, Bartimaeus is asking for the gift that has eluded the
disciples. Would the disciples learn from Bartimaeus, learn that
Jesus' 'authority' was wholly in the service of healing and growth?
'Faith' is confident trust in God and in the healing power of Jesus
(see 5:34). 'Made you well' – saved you – has the same overtones of
salvation as in 5:28, 34. 'Followed him on the way' (v 52) could
mean that the man joined the crowd on their way to Jerusalem. But
Jesus had opened his eyes to a deeper reality. There can be no doubt

that Mark intends: he followed him on the way of Christian discipleship. The phrase 'on the way' and the following of Jesus form an
inclusion with v 32 – 'They were on the road, going up to Jerusalem,
and Jesus was walking ahead of them; they were amazed, and those
who followed were afraid.' Only one of faith, enlightened by Jesus,
one like Bartimaeus, can walk the way of Jesus without consternation and without fear.

Bartimaeus emerges as one of Mark's minor characters – as one of
the most eloquent of them. He was a man of faith who would not be
dissuaded from turning to Jesus in his need. If his initial confession
of Jesus as Son of David was insufficient, though correct,
Bartimaeus, unlike Peter, would not persist in his stubbornness
because Bartimaeus did not 'set his mind on human things' (see
8:33). He came to recognise Jesus and followed him on the way of
discipleship.

B. Jesus in Jerusalem 11:1–13:37

The End of the Temple and its Cult 11:1-25

Jesus' entry into Jerusalem and temple 11:1-11

^{1}When they were approaching Jerusalem, at Bethphage and Bethany, near the mount of Olives, he sent two of his disciples ^{2}and said to them, 'Go into the village ahead of you, and immediately as you enter it, you will find tied there a colt that has never been ridden; untie it and bring it. ^{3}If anyone says to you, 'Why are you doing this?' just say this, 'The Lord needs it and he will send it back here immediately.' ^{4}They went away and found a colt tied near a door, outside in the street. As they were untying it, ^{5}some of the bystanders said to them, 'What are you doing, untying the colt?' ^{6}They told them what Jesus had said; and they allowed them to take it. ^{7}Then they brought the colt to Jesus and threw their cloaks on it; and he sat on it. ^{8}Many people spread their cloaks on the road and others spread leafy branches that they had cut in the fields. ^{9}Then those who went ahead and those who followed were shouting,

Hosanna!
Blessed is the one who comes in the name of the Lord!
Blessed is the coming kingdom of our ancestor David!
Hosanna in the highest heaven!

^{11}Then he entered Jerusalem and went into the temple; and when he had looked around at everything, as it was already late, he went out to Bethany with the twelve.

The fateful journey nears its close. Bethphage and Bethany are the villages nearest Jerusalem on the road from Jericho. Both villages lay on the east slope of the Mount of Olives. The Mount of Olives was, in Jewish expectation, associated with the coming of the Messiah (see Zech 14:4). It is idle to speculate whether the precise directions of Jesus (vv 2-3) indicate a previous arrangement with the owner of the colt. Mark, clearly, presents Jesus as displaying supernatural knowledge in making these arrangements (see 14:13-15).

'The Lord' has need of the colt: the only place in Mark where Jesus is so designated. The title underlines the dominant role of Jesus here.

For Mark's readers the coming of Jesus to Jerusalem had an evident messianic significance. It is not unlikely that the episode happened not at Passover but at a feast of Dedication, and Mark's narrative suggests that it was a modest affair: the immediate disciples and Jesus riding in their midst. Nothing would have been more commonplace than a man riding a donkey; and a small group of pilgrims, waving branches and shouting acclamations from Psalm 118 would not have occasioned a second glance at the feast of Dedication (*Hanukkah*). Yet, whatever others might have thought, those who could see (certainly, Christian readers of the gospel) perceived that this entry to Jerusalem (as it is here presented) was the solemn entry of the Saviour-King into his city. Jesus himself took the initiative: he would enter as the King of Zechariah 9:9 – where it is Yahweh, as divine warrior, who rides into Jerusalem. In Mark there is a studied reticence. The text of Zech 9:9 is not quoted (see Mt 21:5); there are no 'crowds' (Mt 21:9), no 'multitude' (Lk 19:37, 39); the people had not actually acclaimed Jesus as 'Son of David' (see Mt 21:9) thought they had spread their cloaks and leafy branches for his passage.

In this entry to Jerusalem Jesus himself, for the first time in the gospel, made a messianic gesture – but in a special manner, wholly in keeping with his destiny of one who had come to serve and to lay down his life.

Despite the 'many' of v 8, Mark does not give the impression that the accompanying crowd was large; yet they walked before and after Jesus, forming a procession. The entry as depicted in Mark meant the coming of a Messiah who was poor, an advent in humility, not in glory. What was at stake, for Jesus, was the nature and manner of his messiahship. At this moment, come to the city that would so soon witness his passion and death, he could manifest himself. But he did not come as a temporal ruler nor with worldly pomp. He came as a religious figure (in his distinctive understanding of religion), a prince of peace, 'humble and riding on a donkey' (Zech 9:9). Inevitably, he was misunderstood. 'Blessed is the coming kingdom of our father David!': his followers voiced their expectation that he would restore the kingdom of David. Jesus turned from the acclamation. He entered the temple by himself, unobserved; the procession seems to have petered out before the actual entry.

His 'looking around' involved a critical scrutiny which set the stage for the next episode.

The end of the temple 11:12-25

12On the following day, when they came from Bethany, he was hungry.
13Seeing in the distance a fig tree in leaf, he went to see whether perhaps he would find anything on it. When he came to it, he found nothing but leaves, for **it was not the season for figs**. 14He said to it, 'May no one ever eat fruit from you again.'
15Then they came to Jerusalem, and he entered the temple and began to drive out those who were buying in the temple, and he overturned the tables of the money changers and the seats of those who sold doves; 16and he would not allow anyone to carry anything through the temple. 17He was teaching and saying, 'Is it not written, 'My house shall be called a house of prayer for all the nations'? But you have made it a den of robbers'.
18And when the chief priests and the scribes heard it, they kept looking for a way to kill him; for they were afraid of him, because the whole crowd was spellbound by his teaching. 19And when evening came, Jesus and his disciples went out of the city.
20In the morning as they passed by, they saw the fig tree withered away to its roots. 21Then Peter remembered and said to him, 'Rabbi, look! The fig tree that you cursed has withered.' 22Jesus answered them, 'Have faith in God. 23Truly I tell you, if you say to this mountain, "Be taken up and thrown into the sea," and if you do not doubt in your heart, but believe that what you say will come to pass, it will be done for you. 24So I tell you, whatever you ask for in prayer, believe that you have received it, and it will be yours. 25Whenever you stand praying, forgive, if you have anything against anyone; so that your Father in heaven may also forgive you your trespasses.'

It was not the season for figs 11:12-14

An example of Mark's sandwich technique: the account of the cleansing of the temple is inserted between two phases of the other narrative of the fig tree. He thereby signals that the stories should be understood in relation to each other. The cursing (v 21) becomes a judgement on the temple. On the way from Bethany to Jerusalem a leafy tree seemed to promise fruit; but a typically Marcan explanatory phrase explains that 'it was not the season (literally, 'time', *kairos*) for figs.' This jarring note alerts us: we must look to a symbolic meaning: the temple tree, despite its leafy show, is barren at the *kairos* of its visitation. The Messiah 'went to see' and found it fruitless.

But what lies behind this strange story? We may take our choice. Jesus did sentence the fig tree to death; or a parable of his (something like that of Lk 13:6-9) had been turned into a miracle story; or a conspicuous withered tree on the road from Bethany to Jerusalem had given rise to a legend that Jesus had cursed it. For Mark, at any rate, it is a prophetic gesture symbolising the end of the temple and its cult.

Cleansing of the temple 11:15-19
The prophetic gesture of Jesus, his 'cleansing' of the temple, symbolically disrupted the temple's cultic life. He is depicted as driving out those who offered for sale animals and birds and other commodities needed for the sacrifices, the pilgrims who bought from them, and the money-changers who changed the Greek and Roman currency of the pilgrims into the Jewish and Tyrian coinage in which alone the temple tax could be paid. He prohibited the carrying of cultic vessels. It is inconceivable, particularly so near Passsover with its influx of pilgrims, that Jesus could really have cleared the crowded temple courts and brought the whole elaborate business to a standstill. His action, on a necessarily very limited scale, was a prophetic gesture, and would have been recognised as such (v 18).

The motivation of his action is given in v 17. It opens with Marcan emphasis on the teaching of Jesus and runs into a quotation of Is 56:7 with an echo of Jer 7:11. It was God's intention that the temple should be a house of prayer 'for all nations' – of special interest to Mark. This had not been achieved because the temple remained the jealously-guarded preserve of Israel. Worse, the temple and its cult had become a 'den of robbers' as Jer 7: 8-11 makes plain. The temple and its service had become an escape-hatch: the temple cult, it was felt, would automatically win forgiveness of ill behaviour and bring about communion with God. The prophet Jesus was, in this respect, emphatically in the line of Amos, Hosea and Jeremiah (see Amos 4:4-5; 5:21-24; Hosea 5:1-2; 6:1-6; Jeremiah 7:1-15; 26:1-19). In his view, however, because it was so abused, the temple cult had no longer any *raison d'être*. Its time had run out. The prophetic gesture presaged what his death was to achieve (15:38; See 13:2; 14:58; 15:

29). The chief priests and the scribes heard the message (see 11:28). They would not forget.

Coming after the episode of the cleansing of the temple, Peter's drawing of attention to the withered fig tree (vv 20-21) serves to highlight the temple crisis. The verses 22-25 are found in various places in the other gospels. Here they become Mark's comment on the preceding narrative. Temple and its cult are defunct. There is now another way to God, marked by faith (22-23), prayer (24) and forgiveness (25). The saying on forgiveness, which reflects knowledge of the Lord's Prayer (see Mt 6:12) stresses that one cannot pray with hate in one's heart. Mark makes the point that for Jesus' disciples prayer takes the place of temple worship and marks a turn from places and practices that are no longer authentic. There is transition from a reserved temple to a house of prayer for all nations. Jesus is now where God is to be found (see Jn 4:21-23).

The End of Religious Leadership in Israel 11:27–12:44

Controversy 11:27–2: 44

The passage 11:27-33 introduces a series of controversy-stories akin to those in 2:1–3:6. Repeatedly, Jesus reduces to silence the leaders in Israel: chief priests, scribes and elders, Pharisees and Herodians, and Sadducees. Just as in chapter 11 the end of the temple had been marked, so now is shown the end of religious leadership in Israel.

The authority of Jesus 11:27–33

27Again they came to Jerusalem. As he was walking in the temple, the chief priests, the scribes, and the elders came to him 28and said, 'By what authority are you doing these things? Who gave you this authority to do them?' 29Jesus said to them, 'I will ask you one question; answer me, and I will tell you by what authority I do these things. 30Did the baptism of John come from heaven, or was it of human origin? Answer me.' 31They argued with one another, 'If we say, 'From heaven,' he will say, 'Why then did you not believe him?' 32But shall we say, 'Of human origin'?' – they were afraid of the crowd, for all regarded John as truly a prophet. 33So they answered Jesus, 'We do not know.' And Jesus said to them, 'Neither will I tell you by what authority I am doing these things.'

The three groups, chief priests, scribes, and elders are mentioned together as in 8:31; 14:43, 53; 15:1. The point of the question in v 28, referring to his activity in the temple, is to expose a lack of authority on Jesus' part. The matter of the authority of Jesus was also central in 1:27. The authority (*exousia*) in question is not legal or political right but divine authority. In rabbinical fashion, Jesus responds with a counter question which implies that John's authority came from God. He asks his question with insistence. His opponents find themselves trapped. If they acknowledge the heavenly origin of John's authority they convict themselves of unbelief; furthermore, they would have to acknowledge that Jesus' authority, too, is from God. Because of John's standing with the people, they dare not brand him a charlatan. Jesus has effectively rejected their right to challenge him. He has decisively won round one. But, also, he has shown his hand. He has claimed, as they cannot fail to observe, that his authority was from God.

The beloved son 12:1-12
   ¹Then he began to speak to them in parables, 'A man planted a vineyard, put a fence around it, dug a pit for the wine press, and built a watchtower; then he leased it to tenants and went to another country. ²When the season came, he sent a slave to the tenants to collect from them the share of the produce of the vineyard. ³But they seized him, and beat him, and sent him away empty-handed. ⁴And again he sent another slave to them; this one they beat over the head and insulted. ⁵Then he sent another, and that one they killed. And so it was with many others; some they beat, and others they killed. ⁶He had still one other, a beloved son. Finally he sent him to them, saying, 'They will respect my son.' ⁷But these tenants said to one another, 'This is the heir; come, let us kill him, and the inheritance will be ours.' ⁸So they seized him, killed him, and threw him out of the vineyard. ⁹What then will the owner of the vineyard do? He will come and destroy the tenants and give the vineyard to others. ¹⁰Have you not read this scripture:
      The stone that the builders rejected has become the cornerstone;
      ¹¹this was the Lord's doing, and it is amazing in our eyes'?'
   ¹²When they realised that he had told this parable against them, they wanted to arrest him, but they feared the crowd. So they left him and went away.

The allegorical features of the parable of the Wicked Tenants (12:1-12) are evident: the vineyard is Israel, the owner is God, the maltreated servants are God's messengers to Israel, notably the prophets, the beloved son is Jesus. 'Then he began to speak to them in parables' (v 1) – the 'they' are the chief priests, scribes, and elders (see 11:27; 12:12). The Old Testament has a notable instance of a prophet employing a parable with dramatic effect: Nathan's entrapment of David (2 Sam 12:1-7). Mark's parable, too, is dramatic. The description and equipping of the vineyard (Mk 12:1) are based on the allegory of Is 5:1-7 which represents Israel as vineyard of the Lord. Mark's significant modification is to have the landlord let out his vineyard to tenants. It follows that the failure is not on the part of the vineyard (the people) as in Isaiah; the failure is of the tenants, the leaders of the people. And, in its gospel setting, the vineyard is no longer Israel but the larger reality of the kingdom.

The landlord sent his servants to collect his rent, only to have them insulted and maltreated and even killed. He decided to play his last card. He had a beloved son, his only son. He would send him: 'Surely, they will respect my son!' But they killed him and, contemptuously, left him unburied (vv 6-8). So had God dealt with an obdurate people, sending to them, time and again, his servants the prophets. And now, supreme graciousness, he has sent his only Son. This was the ultimate challenge. But the tenants, the leaders, did away with him. Jesus' rhetorical question in v 9 – 'What will the owner of the vineyard do?' – gives punch to the parable; his reply points to judgement on faithless Israel. The tenants, leaders of the covenant people, have brought upon themselves their own dismissal; they have rejected the Son of God (v 9). God looks to others; Mark, likely, has the Gentiles in mind. The parable is aptly in place after 11:12 -21 (prophetic gestures aimed at the temple) and after the question about Jesus' authority (11:27-33). And when there is the question of the alleged rejection of Israel, one must keep in mind the conviction of Paul who, after all, as a fellow Jew, had special affinity with Jesus of Nazareth, that 'all Israel will be saved' (Rom 1:26). Why? On the basis of an impeccable biblical argument: 'The gifts and the calling of God are irrevocable' (11:29).

It is a matter of supreme importance that this parable appears in all three synoptic gospels shortly before their passion narratives. It is a wholly clear indication of how the evangelists understood 'He did not spare his own Son.'

The Father had not thrown his Son to the wolves. The Father had not wished the death of his Son. Father and Son had delivered themselves to the humans they would save. Jesus did not die – Jesus was killed. It was not the Father who killed Jesus.

With the quotation of Ps 118:22-23 in vv 10-11, the figure passes from vineyard to that of building: God's rejected Son has become the cornerstone, the foundation, of the new community. Mark's readers can take heart; they are stones in a building raised by God himself with Jesus Christ as the chief cornerstone (see Eph 2:19-22). In his conclusion (v 12) Mark typically distinguished between the hostile teachers of Israel and the common people who were sympathetic to Jesus (see 11:18). The leaders had caught the drift of the parable only too well (v 12) – 'When they realised that he had told this parable against them, they wanted to arrest him, but they feared the crowd.' They remained 'those outside' (4:11) because they rejected its challenge. They could not bring themselves to acknowledge Jesus. They had rejected the prophet. Now they must silence him.

Question of Pharisees and Herodians 12:13–17

13Then they sent him some Pharisees and some Herodians to trap him in what he said. 14And they came and said to him, 'Teacher, we know that you are sincere, and show deference to no one; for you do not regard people with partiality, but teach the way of God in accordance with truth. Is it lawful to pay taxes to the emperor or not? 15Should we pay them, or should we not?' But, knowing their hypocrisy, he said to them, 'Why are you putting me to the test? Bring me a denarius and let me see it.' 16And they brought one. Then he said to them, 'Whose head is this, and whose title?' They answered, 'The emperor's.' 17Jesus said to them, 'Give to the emperor the things that are the emperor's, and to God the things that are God's.' And they were utterly amazed at him.

This is the finest example of pronouncement story in the gospel – a story which climaxes in a notable saying of Jesus. Everything is subordinated to the pronouncement. As in 3:6, hostile Pharisees and Herodians came 'to trap him in what he said' (12:13). Their flattery – Jesus was an upright teacher who, without pandering to popular opinion or showing partiality, taught steadfastly the way of God – underlined their malicious intent. Ironically, their description of his character and his mission was wholly true. Their trick question bore on the mutual rights of God and of Caesar. The issue was the payment by Jews of a poll tax imposed by Rome. Generally bitterly resented, it was tolerated by Pharisees and, presumably, by Herodians (supporters of Herod Agrippa) since both groups were prepared to go along with the *status quo*. A positive answer by Jesus would be offensive to nationalists; a negative answer would leave him open to being delated to the Romans since non-payment of taxes was tantamount to rebellion. The tax had to be paid in the silver coinage of Tiberius (AD 14-37), a coinage bearing the image of the emperor and the inscription: 'Tiberius Caesar, son of the divine Augustus.' Jesus' request that a coin be produced, and his question, laid the basis of his answer. The validity of one's coinage was coterminous with the range of one's sovereignty. By using the coinage of Caesar, Jews were, *de facto*, acknowledging Caesar's authority and were under obligation to pay taxes to him.

Jesus' answer implies that there need not be conflict between the demands of the state and those of God. The tenor of his teaching made clear his assumption that Caesar's claim would be just: he did not grant Caesar a blank cheque. It must be remembered, however, that he held that the demands of God were all-embracing (see 12: 29-30). Therefore, obligations due to the state fell within the divine order. Jesus disassociated himself from an extreme apocalyptic view (as later expressed in Revelation) which saw the Roman state as wholly evil. There is no evidence of his ever having taken a specific stand against Roman domination. Christians would deduce from Jesus' principle that Christianity could accommodate loyalty to the state. But principle it remained and they had to work out the implications of it. It is not easy always to draw a clear line between a civil sphere where Caesar has his rights and a religious sphere where God rules – if such a distinction makes sense at all. It is not always easy to discern what rightfully belongs to Caesar and where loyalty to the state imposes unacceptable demands. Mark's readers, at least, would have learned from bitter experience that rendering to God the things that are God's had brought them into conflict with the state (13:8-11). Jesus taught no neat doctrine of the relationship of church and state. The church must continue, in changing and fluctuating social and cultural conditions, to sort out its obligations, to discern as honestly as possible what is due to God and what to Caesar. What history shows, unequivocally, is that separation of church and state is absolutely essential.

The Sadducees' Question 12:18-27
    [18]Some Sadducees, who say there is no resurrection, came to him
    and asked him a question, saying, [19]"Teacher, Moses wrote for us

that 'if a man's brother dies, leaving a wife but no child, the man shall marry the widow and raise up children for his brother.' [20]There were seven brothers; the first married and, when he died, left no children; [21]and the second married her and died leaving no children; and the third likewise; [22]none of the seven left children. Last of all the woman herself died. [23]In the resurrection whose wife will she be? For the seven had married her.'
[24]Jesus said to them, 'Is not this the reason you are wrong, that you know neither the scriptures nor the power of God? [25]For when they rise from the dead, they neither marry nor are given in marriage, but are like angels in heaven. [26]And as for the dead being raised, have you not read in the book of Moses, in the story about the bush, how God said to him, 'I am the God of Abraham, the God of Isaac, and the God of Jacob'? [27]He is God not of the dead, but of the living; you are quite wrong.'

The Sadducees were a priestly and aristocratic party whose theology was traditional and conservative. They were not prepared to accept the newfangled doctrine of resurrection (see Acts 23:8). The pronouncement story of 12:18-27 enshrines their objection to it, and Jesus' reply. The case they presented – designed to show that belief in resurrection leads to absurdity – is based on the law of levirate marriage (Deut 25:5-10). The law was in abeyance but could be invoked in theological argument. Jesus' rejoinder was that the Sadducees had not understood the power of God who is capable of achieving something beyond human imagining and, in particular, of making resurrection-life notably different from life on earth. That is the point of the punch-line: 'For when they rise from the dead, they neither marry nor are given in marriage, but are like angels in heaven' (12:25). The statement presents a more sophisticated, as opposed to a popular, notion of resurrection: it will effect a radical transformation.

In vv 26-27 Jesus turned to the fact of resurrection. In Exodus 3:6 Yahweh declared: 'I am ... the God of Abraham, the God of Isaac, and the God of Jacob.' By the time of Moses the three patriarchs had long been dead. And yet, because their God is always God of the living, the patriarchs must, though dead, have been destined for life; they will be raised to life. He had named himself their God, he had made promises to them which could not fail (see Rom 11:29), promises which death could not annul. Their hope of resurrection lay in fellowship with God. By standards of modern exegesis this

rabbinical-style argument is hardly convincing. Yet, the reason proposed for life beyond death is congenial to modern men and
women. 'Proofs' based on the immortality of the soul, presuppos-
ing a questionable dichotomy between 'soul' and 'body', are not
helpful. For the Christian the real ground of immortality is fellowship with the risen Lord and with the living God. Paul has said it
all: 'Thanks be to God who gives us the victory (over death)
through our Lord Jesus Christ' (1 Cor 15:57).

A Scribe's Question 12:28–34

> 28One of the scribes came near and heard them disputing with one
> another, and seeing that he answered them well, he asked him,
> 'Which commandment is the first of all?' 29Jesus answered, 'The
> first is, 'Hear, O Israel: the Lord our God, the Lord is one; 30you shall
> love the Lord your God with all your heart, and with all your soul,
> and with all your mind, and with all your strength.' 31The second is
> this, 'You shall love your neighbour as yourself.' There is no other
> commandment greater than these.' 32Then the scribe said to him,
> 'You are right, Teacher; you have truly said that 'he is one, and
> besides him there is no other'; 33and 'to love him with all the heart,
> and with all the understanding, and with all the strength', and 'to
> love one's neighbour as oneself,' – this is much more important than
> all whole burnt offerings and sacrifices.' 34When Jesus saw that he
> answered wisely, he said to him, 'You are not far from the kingdom
> of God.' After that no one dared to ask him any question.

In another pronouncement story, Jesus gives the answer to the
question, 'Which commandment is the first of all?' It was a question
the rabbis sought to answer. They looked for the commandment
that outweighed all the others, one that might be regarded as a
basic principle on which the whole law was grounded. We find
something of this in Matthew's declaration: 'On these two commandments hang all the law and the prophets' (Mt 22:40). Because
it is an honest question by one well-disposed (vv 32-34) Jesus
answers directly. He begins by quoting the opening formula (Deut
6: 4) of the *Shema*, the 'creed' which every male Israelite recited
morning and evening, and joined to it Lev 19:18 on the love of the
neighbour. He had been asked to name the first commandment; he
responds by naming two commandments. This is of great importance. It would seem that Jesus was the first to bring together these
two commands of love of God and love of neighbour. That is,
because for him, the one flows directly, and necessarily, from the

other. Love for neighbour arises out of love for God. He had taken and welded the two precepts into one.

In the synoptic gospels, only here and in Lk 11:42, is there word of humans' love for God, and it appears sparingly in the rest of the New Testament. Usually, the emphasis is on God's love for humankind. And this is as it should be. It is because God has first loved us that we love God (Rom 5:5,8; 1 Jn 4:11). Indeed, love for one another is the test of the reality of our love of God (1 Jn 4:20-21). Jesus himself showed in his life and death the quality of this twofold love. His love for God motivated his total dedication to his mission; his love for humankind marked him as one who had come to serve the saving purpose of God, one who had laid down his life as a ransom for humanity (10:45).

The scribe's reply (vv 32-33) is proper to Mark. He agrees fully with Jesus' answer and further specifies that the true love of God and the loving service of others is more important than elaborate cult. His insistence on love with the whole heart is a recognition that love cannot be measured. Love is incompatible with a legalism that sets limits, that specifies what one should do and should avoid. Jesus' assurance that this scribe is not far from the kingdom of God is, in truth, an invitation. And we sense that this time the invitation will not be in vain (see 10:17-23). Nowhere else in the gospels does a scribe emerge in such a favourable light.

This is the end of the questioning of Jesus (v 34b). One does not long engage in debate with him. Meeting with Jesus is too radical an experience: one must quickly come to a decision, to accept or to reject. It is now Jesus' turn to ask his question.

Jesus' Question 12:35-37a
35While Jesus was teaching in the temple, he said, 'How can the scribes say that the Messiah is the son of David? 36David himself, by the Holy Spirit, declared,

> The Lord said to my Lord, 'Sit at my right hand,
> until I put your enemies under your feet.'

37aDavid himself calls him Lord; so how can he be his son?'

It might seem that Jesus' question is designed to contest the Davidic descent of the Messiah. Rather, it is meant as a refutal of the scribes' understanding of Davidic messiahship. Psalm 110, the opening verse of which is quoted here, is a royal psalm, addressed to the king – 'my lord' refers to the king. Sitting at the right hand of God means the king's adoption as God's son, the acknowledged status of the Davidic king (2 Sam 7:14). The argument here depends on the current acceptance of the psalm as a composition of David (it is, in fact, later). On this supposition David presents an oracle of God addressed to one whom he entitles 'my Lord'. This solemn attestation of David is underlined by the formula, unique in the synoptics, 'by the Holy Spirit'. This adds weight to the further question in v 37: if the great David addresses the Messiah as 'Lord' then the Davidic sonship of the Messiah must be understood in a sense that will acknowledge his superiority to David.

It is at this point in his gospel, the very end of the mission, that Mark has raised directly the issue of the rightful meaning of the messianic title, Son of David. In 10:45-48 he had Jesus addressed as 'Son of David' and had offered no comment, apart from Jesus' own brief appearance as the humble prince of Zechariah (11:1-10). But now he intimates that this title, like everything about Jesus, can be understood only when his messianic status is revealed through the death and resurrection of the Son of Man.

The false religion of the scribes 12:37b-44

37b And the large crowd was listening to him with delight. 38 As he taught, he said, 'Beware of the scribes, who like to walk around in long robes, and to be greeted with respect in the marketplaces, 39 and to have the best seats in the synagogues and places of honour at banquets! 40 They devour widows' houses and for the sake of appearance say long prayers. They will receive the greater condemnation.'

41 He sat down opposite the treasury, and watched the crowd putting money into the treasury. Many rich people put in large sums. 42 A poor widow came and put in two small copper coins, which are worth a penny. 43 Then he called his disciples and said to them, 'Truly I tell you, this poor widow has put in more than all those who are contributing to the treasury. 44 For all of them have contributed out of their abundance; but she out of her poverty has put in everything she had, all she had to live on.'

The gospel presentation of scribes paints them, in our terms, as theologians and lawyers. They prided themselves on their expertise and on their meticulous religious observance. On both scores they (or some among them) invited and received deference; to that end they affected distinctive dress (see Mt 23:1-7).

It ought surely be of more than academic interest that the Jesus-tradition is critical of 'churchly' dress and 'ecclesiastical' lifestyle. The scribes claimed the 'best seats' in the synagogues: directly in front of the ark containing the sacred scrolls and facing the people. The charge of v 40 is more serious: 'They devour widows' houses and for the sake of appearance say long prayers.' In other words, they are accused of exploiting the social and financial vulnerability of widows. Judaism had some scathing condemnation of unscrupulous scribes. The sweeping tone of the charges here, however, reflects the animosity between the church and official Judaism, an animosity more trenchantly expressed in Matthew 23.

This portrait of the scribes stands, and was meant to stand, in sharp contrast to the attitude and conduct of Christian leaders (9:33-37; 10:42-45). What has been and continues to be, the reality in the church? Distinctive dress, honorific titles, signs of deference, places of honour at religious and civic functions! It is not easy to see a difference between such practice and the conduct of the scribes outlined and censured here in vv 38-39.

The vignette of The Widow's Mite (vv 41-44) may have found its setting here partly because of the catchword 'widow' (vv 40, 42). More to the point, Jesus' previous castigation of scribes as those who 'devour widows' houses' is surely in mind. The 'copper coin' (*lepton*) was the smallest in circulation.

Mention of two coins is important: the woman might have kept one for herself. Instead, she put in both, 'all she had to live on'. This poor widow was a victim of religious establishment. She had been convinced that it was a 'holy' thing to give her all to the temple. She is a tragic example of a situation Jesus had in mind when he declared: 'Religion is for men and women, not men and women for religion' (see 2:27).

The traditional understanding of the passage is very different. The widow is representative of genuine Jewish piety in contrast to the counterfeit piety of the scribes (or, of scribes characterised in vv 38-39). Wealthy people had been generous (v 41). This poor widow's mite was an immeasurably greater gift than theirs, for she had given of her all – her 'whole living' (v 44). She had let go of every shred of security and had committed herself wholly to God. Indeed,

Mark seems to take it in this sense. The nagging question remains. Jesus appears to commend a practically penniless widow for her action of donating to a wealthy temple all she had to sustain her very life; indeed he implicitly presents her as a model. She would give everything she had – and starve! Is this compatible with Jesus' distinctive concern for the poor and marginalized? I think not. Jesus has reduced to silence the religious authorities of Israel. The only authority left is that of the Son of Man, the one come to serve and to offer his life for all (see 10: 45).

Farewell Discourse Mark 13

This chapter, which concludes the narrative of the mission of Jesus and, in view of his departure from this world, prepares the disciples for events yet to come, falls into the literary form of farewell discourse. We find this form in the Old Testament, e.g. Deut 31-32 (Moses); 1 Chron 28-29 (David); and in the New Testament, Jn 13:31 –16: 33 (Jesus) and Acts 20:17-35 (Paul). While presented as the farewell discourse of Jesus, the chapter is a thoroughly Marcan construct, incorporating traditional material. It has close contacts with what goes before and what is to come.

Structure of Mark 13

Introduction 13:1-4
I. *The End of Jerusalem 13:5-23*
A 13:5-6 False prophets
   B 13:7-8 Wars and rumours of wars
      C 13:9-13 Persecution and Mission
   B' 13:14-20 Wars and rumours of wars
A' 13:21-23 False prophets
II. *The End of the World 13:24-27*
Sign of the Coming of the Son of Man 13:24-27
The signs of the End 13:28-36
a. Parable of the fig tree 13:28-29
   b. Saying: 'This generation ...' 13:30
      c. Solemn confirmation 13:31
   b'. Saying: 'About that day or hour ...' 13:32
a'. Parable of the doorkeeper 13:33-36
Conclusion. 'Keep awake' 13:37

¹As he came out of the temple, one of his disciples said to him, 'Look, Teacher, what large stones and what large buildings!' ²Then Jesus asked him, 'Do you see these great buildings? Not one stone will be left here upon another; all will be thrown down.' ³When he was sitting on the Mount of Olives opposite the temple, **Peter, James, John, and Andrew** asked him privately, ⁴'Tell us, when will this be, and what will be the sign that **all these things** are about to be accomplished?' ⁵Then Jesus began to say to them, '**Beware** that no one leads you astray. ⁶Many will come in my name and say, 'I am he!' and they will lead many astray. ⁷When you hear of wars and rumours of wars, do not be alarmed; this must take place, but the end is still to come. ⁸For nation will rise against nation, and kingdom against kingdom; there will be earthquakes in various places; there will be famines. This is but the beginning of the birthpangs.'

⁹'As for yourselves, **beware**; for they will **hand you over** to councils; and you will be beaten in synagogues; and you will stand before governors and kings because of me, as a testimony to them. ¹⁰And the good news must first be proclaimed to all nations. ¹¹When they bring you to trial and **hand you over**, do not worry beforehand about what you are to say; but say whatever is given you at that time, for it is not you who speak, but the Holy Spirit. ¹²Brother **will betray** brother to death, and a father his child, and children will rise against parents and have them put to death; ¹³and you will be hated by all because of my name. But the one who endures to the end will be saved.

¹⁴But when you see the devastating sacrilege set up where it ought not to be (let the reader understand), then those in Judea must flee to the mountains; ¹⁵the one on the housetop must not go down or enter the house to take anything away; ¹⁶the one in the field must not turn back to get a coat. ¹⁷Woe to those who are pregnant and to those who are nursing infants in those days! ¹⁸Pray that it may not be in winter. ¹⁹For in those days there will be suffering, such as has not been since the beginning of the creation that God created until now, no, and never will be. ²⁰And if the Lord had not cut short those days, no one would be saved; but for the sake of the elect, whom he chose, he has cut short those days. ²¹And if anyone says to you at that time, 'Look! Here is the Messiah!' or 'Look! There he is!' – do not believe it. ²²False messiahs and false prophets will appear and produce signs and omens, to lead astray, if possible, the elect. ²³But **be alert**; I have already told you everything . ²⁴But in those days, after that suffering, the sun will be darkened, and the moon will not give its light ²⁵and the stars of heaven will be falling from heaven, and the powers in the heavens will be shaken.

²⁶Then they will see 'the Son of man coming in clouds' with great power and glory. ²⁷Then he will send out the angels, and gather his elect from the four winds, from the ends of the earth to the ends of heaven.

²⁸From the fig tree learn its lesson: as soon as its branch becomes tender and puts forth its leaves, you know that summer is near. ²⁹So also, when you see these things taking place, you know that he is near, at the very gates. ³⁰Truly I tell you, this generation will not pass away until **all these things** will have taken place. ³¹Heaven and earth will pass away, but my words will not pass away.

³²But about that day or hour no one knows, neither the angels in heaven, nor the Son, but only the Father. ³³**Beware, keep alert,** for you do not know when the time will come. ³⁴It is like a man going on a journey, when he leaves home and puts his slaves in charge, each with his work, and commands the doorkeeper to be on the watch. ³⁵Therefore, **keep awake** – for you do not know when the master of the house will come, in the evening, or at midnight, or at cockcrow, or at dawn, ³⁶or else he may find you asleep when he comes suddenly. ³⁷And what I say to you I say to all: **Keep awake**.'

Introduction 13:1-4

Mark has been preoccupied with the temple since 11:11 when Jesus came to it in judgement and, with prophetic gestures (11:12-25), had heralded its end. If he now leaves the temple it is to forecast its destruction (vv 1-2); and Jerusalem is never again mentioned by name in this gospel (see 14: 13). As he left the temple a disciple drew Jesus' attention to what was, in truth, the grandeur of the Herodian temple, for Herod's temple was one of the most remarkable buildings of its time. Jesus' response is a grim prediction of the total destruction of the magnificent building; it spells out in clear words what was implied in the fig-tree episode (11:12-14, 20-21).

The carefully designed setting (vv 3-4) admirably lends to this discourse the solemnity and extraordinary importance that Mark wants it to have. In Zech 14:4 the Mount of Olives is associated with an oracle of judgement on Jerusalem. Jesus is enthroned upon the mountain and looking down on the doomed city. The discourse is not only 'in private', it is reserved for four of the twelve, the four whose call is described in 1:16-20 – and who have been longest with Jesus. Mark has thus alerted the reader that this reply to the disciples' question is of exceptional moment. And so indeed it was for Mark's community Already the question (v 4) evokes the fuller significance of the end of the temple. It is a two-fold question regarding the when of these things (*tauta*) – the destruction of the temple (v 2), and the sign that will precede the accomplishment of all these things (*tauta panta*) – the End. In this manner, the end of the temple is associated with the end of all things. And this, indeed, would seem to be the problem involved. Christians, already convinced of an imminent *parousia*, would, very naturally, link that hope to the grim events of the Jewish War (66-70AD), a fitting scenario for the End. Expectation would have heightened as the crisis sharpened. And then came their shock and bewilderment when the end of the city did not, after all, usher in the End (see 9:2-9). This is why the discourse focuses on the *parousia* (vv 24-27) and its nearness (vv 28-36), and fits the war, the end of the temple, and the contemporary trials of Christians into the category of preliminary signs (vv 5-23).

I. The End of Jerusalem 13:5-23

False prophets 13:5-6 [21-23]
The discourse begins with a note of warning, 'Beware' (*blepete*), v 5b, which corresponds to the conclusion of v 21: 'Do not believe.' The warning is about many who would lead others astray. They will come in Jesus' name declaring 'I am he!' These deceivers are more clearly designated in the corresponding v 22 as 'false messiahs and false prophets' who declared that they knew where the Messiah would appear (v 21). These must be Christians who invoked the authority and even assumed the identity of Jesus. We know that in Judaism at the time there was intense messianic expectation, fomented by the events of the war, and more than one messianic claimant had won a following. It is not surprising that some Christians, too, would have been carried away.

Wars and rumours of wars 13:7-8
'Wars and rumours of wars' had become commonplace in apocalyptic descriptions of the end of the world; they were regarded as a necessary feature of a divine purpose – 'this must take place'; see Dan 2:28). The grim experience of war conditions in Palestine would have been aggravated by rumours of wars and disasters throughout the Empire. These rumours would fuel the conviction of the fanatics that now indeed was the moment of the inbreaking of the kingdom, now was the time of the End. Mark challenges this interpretation and insists that the hour is but the beginning of the 'birthpangs', a traditional term to express the view that the messianic age would come to birth through a period of woes. We shall see that the corresponding verses (14-20) describe these events in greater detail. Christians are assured that these upheavals are, after

all, but the first pains of childbirth. However, they do know that they live in 'the beginning of the birthpangs', and the warning of v 9 is sounded.

Persecution and mission 13:9-13

The admonition to beware (v 9) marks a transition to this central section of the chiasm which deals with the hard lot of Christians. Noteworthy is the threefold repetition of 'to deliver up' (vv 9b, 11a, 12a): persecution and suffering are their lot, as for their Master. They will be hauled before Jewish tribunals (v 9a) and Gentile authorities (v 9b). Paradoxically, these Christians, though in the guise of arraigned prisoners, will be bearing witness to the Name. Even more strangely – for God's ways are not the ways of humankind – persecution will be the occasion of the wider mission to the Gentiles (v 10; see Acts 8:1-5). For that matter, one may say that Christian suffering is itself that proclamation: by suffering as Jesus suffered, they are making him present to their world. For Mark, it is wholly fitting that the suffering and death of Christians should open the way to the Gentiles. Already he had shown that the death of the precursor had coincided with the first sending of the Twelve on their mission (6:7-30). He will show that the death of Jesus tears away the veil of division between Jew and Gentile (15:38). Moreover, by asserting that the gospel must 'first' be preached, Mark is asserting that the gathering in of the full number of the Gentiles (see Rom 11:35) is part of God's plan. Hence this present suffering of Christians does not mark the End. In their trials Christians are assured of help (v 11). It is not said that the Spirit will speak up on behalf of the disciples. Rather, they are assured of the help of the Spirit; and the preparation of the defence is less the drafting of an *apologia* than a prayer. Here is a sign and a promise of God's help in trouble.

Wars and rumours of wars 13:14- 20

The solemn setting of the discourse, we have seen (v 3), has alerted the reader to its exceptional importance. If, then, Mark still finds it necessary to further nudge the reader ('let the reader understand', v 14), it can only because he wants to drop a dark hint, to point the Christian reader to a hidden clue. We are to look to the meaning of 'the desolating sacrilege' which, at first sight, does not seem to offer much of a riddle. The phrase (more familiarly, 'the abomination of desolation') comes from Daniel (Dan 9:27; 11:31; 12:11) where it refers to the heathen altar which Antiochus Epiphanes built over the temple altar of burnt offering in 168BC (see 1 Macc 1: 54), thereby radically profaning the temple – in effect, 'destroying' it. It would, then, be an apt expression to describe the destruction of Herod's temple in 70AD. The puzzling feature is that Mark speaks of this 'desolating sacrilege' in personal terms: the Greek participle *hestékota* is masculine. This mysterious person is standing where he should not be, that is, in the temple. It seems probable that the reference is to Titus, who brought Roman standards into the temple area and was acclaimed as emperor there. This clearly implies the capture of the city. The command to flee (14b-19) must, originally, regard an earlier time, before the Roman assault of the city, when flight was still possible.

That Mark is looking beyond the historical end of Jerusalem is clear in vv 19-20. The Jerusalem disaster is but the first moment of unparalelled tribulation that will involve the whole of creation (v 19) – 'those days' points to that eschatological time of tribulation. The feature of the shortening of the days of tribulation (v 20) expresses the idea that God, in his mercy, and for the sake of his elect, shortens the period of tribulation for humankind. Notice the comforting emphasis: 'the elect whom he chose' (v 20), that is, the Christian community. The false prophets reappear, making false messianic claims. There is the comfort that they will not succeed in leading astray faithful Christians precisely because they are 'the elect whom he chose'. And there is the note of warning: 'be alert' (*blepete*), echoing the opening word of Jesus (v 5) and tying together this whole section.

II. The end of the World 13:24 -27

Mark certainly believes in a *parousia* (advent) of the Son of Man and is convinced that it is imminent; in this he shows the common expectation of early Christians. The passage vv 24-27 is a collage of prophetic texts. The cosmic signs which accompany the *parousia* (vv 24-25) are part and parcel of Jewish apocalyptic descriptions of the day of the Lord. The *parousia* marks the definitive manifestation of the Son of Man. Then he will be seen in fullness instead of being dimly perceived. This is the real message of hope for Christians. This promise and this hope they cling to while the Lord is absent

(2:20; 13:34). It is this that enables them, no matter what their present situation, to endure to the end (13:9-13). Already 8:38 had warned that only those who, here and now, in this vale of tears, are not 'ashamed' of a suffering Son of Man will rejoice in his glorious coming. That is why Mark will go on, insistently, to urge watching and readiness for the coming (vv 33-37). And, for the faithful ones, the coming will be joy indeed. The Son of Man will not come to execute judgement. The one purpose of his appearing will be to gather his elect. After his comforting presentation of the *parousia*, Mark develops that encouragement by stressing its nearness. But he insists that the intervening time must be spent in watchfulness (vv 28-32). There can never be room for complacency in the life of the Christian.

The Signs of the End 13:28-31

The fig tree emerges again (13:28-29; see 11:12-14) but now as a parabolic promise of the nearness of the coming of the Son of Man. It helps to answer the question: How soon is the *parousia*? A fig tree is singled out because in Palestine, where most trees are evergreen, the appearance of leaves or buds on the fig tree is a sure sign of the end of winter and the beginning of summer. The 'when' of v 29 echoes the 'when' of vv 7, 11, 14 and implies the answer to the twofold question of v 4. The first part of that double question is answered in v 29. When Christians see the destruction of the temple and its possession by the desolating sacrilege they will know that the prediction of Jesus had come true. Then, too, they will know that the coming of the Son of Man is near. As to when 'all these things are about to be accomplished' (v 4) – the end will come in 'this generation', that of Mark himself; the Son of Man is 'at the very gates' indeed (v 29). The evangelist has left us in no doubt as to his conviction. The *parousia* will occur in his own lifetime; or, at least, his generation will not have quite passed away before the End comes. His ultimate assurance is not founded on the end of the temple but is anchored in the authority of the words of Jesus (v 31). The End will be after the destruction of the temple (which had already happened) and in his generation – of this Mark is sure. But he will not specify day or hour, because he cannot. For that matter, not even the members of the heavenly court (the angels), not even the Son himself, know the precise date of the End – the Son and the angels who are the protagonists of the *parousia* (13:26-27). It remains the secret of the Father.

There can be no doubt that Mark expected an imminent *parousia*. Was he, then, mistaken? In one sense, obviously, yes; the *parousia* of the Son of Man did not happen in his generation, nor has it occurred twenty centuries later. Yet, we can find a basic truth in Mark's conviction. The death and resurrection of Christ did usher in the last age. Besides, '*parousia*' is an apocalyptic symbol which gives dramatic expression to the belief that God's saving plan is perfectly rounded. While we cannot share Mark's view that the End is very near, nor look for a coming of the Son of Man in clouds, we do share his faith in God's victory in Christ. And, for each of us, the '*parousia*' will be our meeting with the Son of Man when we pass out of this life into the life of God. It should be our Christian hope that we stand among the elect to be fondly welcomed by him.

The exhortation of v 33 is Mark's introduction to the parable of the doorkeeper (vv 34-36). 'Beware' (vv 5, 9, 23, 33) is the keynote of the farewell discourse. 'Keep alert' means do not permit yourself to fall asleep! 'Time' (*kairos*) is the appointed time fixed in an ordered divine plan. In its context the 'time' refers to the incalculable 'day or hour', of v 32; the End is near – but cannot be marked on a calendar. The call to watchfulness in v 33 brings out the exhortation latent in v 32.

The parable of the doorkeeper, as Mark found it, had already gone through a process of reshaping. It certainly resembles the Watching Servants of Lk 12:35-38 – indeed both should be regarded as widely variant forms of the same parable. The main sentence of v 35, 'Therefore, keep awake ... or else he may find you asleep when he comes suddenly', is the application of the parable. Significantly, it is 'the master of the house' who will come, not the 'man' of v 34; it is Christ himself. The parable is now understood in christological terms. Christ is the departing Lord and the *parousia* will mark his return. The doorkeeper represents the waiting disciples, the community of believers, and the divisions of the night are a symbol for the lapse of time before the coming. This meaning is borne out by Mark's care to bracket the first part of the parable with the warnings, 'for you do not know when the time will come' (v 33b), 'for you do not know when the master of the house will come' (v 35b).

The opening 'Beware' (v 5) and the final 'Keep awake' (v 37) emphasise that Mark's real interest in this passage is centred in the exhortation, and his lesson is for all Christians without exception: 'I say to all.' The repeated call to watchfulness indicates how he wanted, not only this parable but the whole discourse, to be understood: not as a guide in calculating a deadline, but as an inspiration and a warning, to live one's life at each moment in preparedness for the meeting with Christ.

C. The Passion of Jesus 14:1–15:47

After the farewell discourse the curtain goes up on the final act of the drama. We have been well prepared for the denouement, not only in the explicit predictions of the passion, but in hints, more or less veiled, right from the beginning. The Son of Man must suffer many things. In this divine necessity Mark finds his reply to the question: Who, then, is this? The precise answer is spoken by the centurion: 'Truly, this man was God's Son!' But the whole gospel has prepared for that solemn declaration

Marked for Death 14:1-11

[1]It was two days before the Passover and the festival of Unleavened Bread. The chief priests and the scribes were looking for a way to arrest Jesus by stealth and kill him, [2]for they said, 'Not during the festival, or there may be a riot among the people.'

[3]While he was at Bethany in the house of Simon the leper, as he sat at the table, a woman came with an alabaster jar of very costly ointment of nard, and she broke open the jar and poured the ointment on his head. [4]But some were there who said to one another in anger, 'Why was the ointment wasted in this way? [5]For this ointment could have been sold for more than three hundred denarii, and the money given to the poor.' And they scolded her. [6]But Jesus said, 'Let her alone; why do you trouble her? She has performed a good service for me. [7]For you always have the poor with you, and you can show kindness to them whenever you wish; but you will not always have me. [8]She has done what she could; she has anointed my body beforehand for its burial. Truly I tell you, wherever the good news is proclaimed in the whole world, what she has done will be told in remembrance of her.'

[10]Then Judas Iscariot, who was one of the twelve, went to the chief priests in order **to betray him** to them. [11]When they heard it, they were greatly pleased, and promised to give him money. So he began to look for an opportunity **to betray him**.

The feast of Passover began at sundown. That moment marked the beginning of 15 Nisan by Jewish liturgical reckoning of the day (sundown to sundown). The lambs had been slaughtered and

offered in the temple on the late afternoon (that is, 14 Nisan); the
meal followed between sundown and midnight (15 Nisan). The
Feast of Unleavened Bread, originally a feast of the barley harvest
during which unleavened bread was eaten, was celebrated from 15
to 21 Nisan. The two feasts had become combined and Mark's designation (Passover and Feast of Unleavened Bread) was not unusual.
The precise 'two days', a feature of Mark's concern with time division throughout the passion narrative, alerts one to a divine purpose
in all that is to transpire. Hostile action against Jesus, long before
made explicit (3:6), now looks for its moment: the Jewish leaders
plot the death of Jesus (vv 1-2). Yet, even here, God has his say: 'Not
during the feast' – so decreed human prudence. But Jesus did die
during the festival! The Pharisees have disappeared from the story.
It is not they but the temple priests who brought about the death of
Jesus.

She has done a beautiful thing to me 14:3-9

The sequel to the priests' plot is obviously Judas' betrayal (vv 10-
11). The intercalated anointing scene is thereby highlighted by
Mark and is meant to be understood in the context of that frame-
work. This story of the anointing is located at Bethany (v 11) in the
house of 'Simon the leper,' doubtless one known in the circle where
the story originated. The woman is not named; interest falls on the
words of Jesus (vv 7-9). She is, obviously, a disciple – how else
might one account for her gesture? Her anointing was, implicitly, a
royal anointing. Jesus graciously accepted anointing but related it
to his death. This woman had made a lovely gesture, more meaningful than she knew; she, the woman disciple, showed an understanding that the men disciples lacked (see Mt 26:8). Her gracious
deed will win her immortality: 'Truly I tell you, wherever the good
news is proclaimed in the whole world, what she has done will be
told in remembrance of her' (v 9). The deed of this woman is firmly
highlighted. But what has happened to the story in Christian tradition? Has that 'lovely deed' become a prominent feature in the
gospel knowledge of Christians? She has remained in her marginal
anonymity. Poignantly, the lovely gesture of this unknown woman
stands between the deadly intent of the priests and the betrayal of
Jesus by a disciple. Priests and scribes were wondering how they
might arrest Jesus 'by stealth'; now, unexpectedly, an occasion is

presented to them. But there is nothing fortuitous about it. The verb translated 'betray' is, literally, 'to deliver up,' practically a technical term for a delivering up which is God's will: Judas is serving a divine purpose (see v 21). Mark's reticence is noteworthy. He offers no explanation of the treachery (see Lk 22:3; Jn 12:6; 13:27). Nor does Judas strike a bargain with the priests as in Mt 26:15; he receives no more than a promise of money for his pains. While it is true that Judas is consistently described in the gospel tradition as 'one of the twelve', that designation has special urgency here. The bitterness of the fate of Jesus is beginning to emerge.

The Farewell Supper 14:12-25

12On the first day of Unleavened Bread, when the Passover lamb is sacrificed, his disciples said to him, 'Where do you want us to go and make the preparations for you to eat the Passover?' 13So he sent two of his disciples, saying to them, 'Go into the city, and a man carrying a jar of water will meet you; follow him, 14and wherever he enters, say to the owner of the house, 'The Teacher asks, Where is my guest room where I may eat the Passover with my disciples?' 15He will show you a large room upstairs, furnished and ready. Make preparations for us there.' 16So the disciples set out and went to the city , and found everything as he had told them; and they prepared the Passover meal.
17When it was evening, he came with the twelve. 18And when they had taken their places and were eating, Jesus said, 'Truly I tell you, one of you **will betray me**, one who is eating with me.' 19They began to be distressed and to say to him one after another, 'Surely, not I?' 20He said to them, 'It is one of the twelve, one who is dipping bread into the bowl with me. 21For the Son of Man goes as it is written of him, but woe to that one by whom the Son of man **is betrayed**! It would have been better for that one not to have been born.'
22While they were eating, he took a loaf of bread, and after blessing it he broke it, gave it to them, and said, 'Take; this is my body.' 23Then he took a cup, and after giving thanks he gave it to them, and all of them drank from it. 24He said to them, 'This is my blood of the covenant, which is poured out for many. 25Truly I tell you, I will never again drink of the fruit of the vine until that day when I drink it new in the kingdom of God.

The account of preparation for the farewell meal (14:12-16) is quite like that of preparation for the entry to Jerusalem (11:1-6). Here, as there, two disciples are sent off with a precise description of the situation they will encounter and are told exactly what to say. And here, too, all turned out as the Teacher had assured them. Here only

in Mark is the last supper designated a Passover meal. In fact, the
Last Supper was a solemn farewell meal – not a traditional passover
meal.

Between preparation for the Supper and the Supper itself the evangelist intercalated the announcement-of-betrayal passage (vv 17-
21). Jesus' opening words (v 18) echo Ps 41:9: 'Even my bosom
friend in whom I trusted, who ate of my bread, has lifted his heel
against me.' His words, 'one who is eating with me ... dipping
bread into the bowl with me', express the horror of treachery in the
sacred setting of table fellowship. There is the added awfulness: it is
one of the Twelve. Shattering though it be, betrayal was in accordance with the divine plan for the passion: 'as it is written'.

Judas, mysteriously, had served a divine purpose. He aided the
priests in their plan to arrest Jesus 'by stealth' by leading the arresting band to where Jesus was and by identifying him (14:43-45). His
part in this must be, basically, as historical as Peter's denials of
Jesus. In each case one of the Twelve had acted discreditably – conduct that could not be denied. In Mark, however, Judas' deed is not
overly stressed. This is so despite the statement of v 21. Commonly
this has been read as a curse on Judas – even implying his damn-
ation. The saying is a 'woe', not a 'curse'; these are distinct literary
types. To interpret the woe as a curse is a serious misunderstanding
of the text. The proper meaning is well expressed by Vincent
Taylor: 'the "Woe" pronounced over him [Judas] is not a curse, but
a cry of sorrow and of anguish: "Alas! For that man," and the saying, "It were better, etc," is not a threat, but a sad recognition of
facts.' (*The Gospel According to St Mark*, 2nd ed, London: Macmillan,
1966, 542). The phrase 'as it is written of him' conveys the same idea
as 'delivered up' – divine purpose. What was written was that the
Son of Man 'goes': death was accepted by Jesus himself. And
behind it all is a chastening admonishment to the reader. Mark has
placed the betrayal episode in the setting of eucharistic table fellowship. The Christian must ask: 'Is it I? – am I a betrayer of the Lord
Jesus?' (see v 19). One is reminded of Paul in 1 Cor 11:28: 'Examine
yourselves, and only then eat of the bread and drink of the cup.'

The phrase 'While they were eating' (v 22) resumes the meal
episode after the warning of betrayal (vv 17-21). Jesus 'took bread',
'blessed', 'broke', 'gave'; the same actions and the very same words

as in both feeding stories (6:41; 8:6). Then the disciples 'did not understand about the loaves' (6:52; see 8:17-21); now the mystery is being revealed. Jesus is the 'one loaf' for Jews and Gentiles because, as he tells them, his body is being given and his blood poured out for Jew and Gentile, 'for many [=all]' (vv 23-24).

'This is my body': Paul (1 Cor 11:22) adds 'which is for you'. But this is already firmly implied in Mark both through the repeated references to Jesus' death since the beginning of the passion narrative and the explicit statement in the cup saying: 'This is my blood of the covenant.' Exodus 24:8 is certainly in mind: 'See the blood of the covenant that the Lord has made with you.' By the sprinkling of sacrificial blood the people of Israel shared in the blessings of the covenant given at Sinai. Likewise this blood of the cup will be poured out 'for many' (a Semitism, meaning 'all'): a new covenant is being forged and sealed whose blessings are offered to all. The death of Jesus founds the new community. The Last Supper helps us to understand the meaning of Jesus' death on Calvary.

The Supper narrative (vv 22-25) is based on the eucharistic liturgical tradition of Mark's community. While less explicit than the Pauline tradition (1 Cor 11:23-26) it has the same meaning. In both, the body and blood seals a new covenant. In both, the eucharistic meal anticipates the eschatological banquet of the kingdom. And if Mark does not have Paul's 'Do this in remembrance of me', the eucharistic liturgy of his church was the living fulfilment of that word.

Prediction of failure 14:26-31
26. When they had sung the hymn, they went out to the Mount of Olives. [27]And Jesus said to them, 'You will all become deserters; for it is written, 'I will strike the shepherd, and the sheep will be scattered.' [28]But after I am raised up, I will go before you to Galilee.' [29]Peter said to him, 'Even though all become deserters, I will not.' [30]Jesus said to him, 'Truly I tell you, this day, this very night, before the cock crows twice, you will deny me three times.' [31]But he said vehemently, 'Even though I must die with you, I will not deny you.' And all of then said the same.

In the quotation from Zechariah one finds the key to Mk 14:27-28. After declaring, 'strike the shepherd, that the sheep may be scattered' (Zech 13:7) the oracle goes on to declare that two-thirds of the shepherd-king's people will perish (13:8). The remnant will be refined and tested to become truly God's people (13:9). Jesus gives assurance that his community, too, though scattered following the fate of their shepherd, will be reconstituted by him. He looks beyond his death and promises that the scattered flock will be gathered together again. 'After I am raised up, I will go before you to Galilee' (Mk 14:28). The phrase, 'I will go before you' could be taken as 'I will lead you' or 'I will go there beforehand'. Either way, the disciples will meet Jesus again in Galilee (see 16:7). It would be a rebirth for them, a new beginning. 'Galilee' will be, again, the area of mission – of universal mission (see 13:10).

Peter is a leader and his example is infectious. Now all the others, a moment ago filled with consternation (v 19), find new courage. They, too, are quite ready to die for their Master (v 31). That is as it should be, for Mark has repeatedly emphasised that Jesus' suffering and the suffering of his disciples go hand in hand (8:31, 34-38; 9: 31; 10:32-34, 39, 52). They will learn that this cannot be their doing but is a gift of grace. It can only be because Jesus had gone before.

Gethsemane 14:32-42

Mark's story takes a dramatic turn. We had become accustomed to the idea of Jesus' death. We have been given clues, particularly in 10:33-34, a few pages back. We have come to expect that Jesus will go, unruffled, to meet his fate (see 10:32). We could not be prepared for what the evangelist has to tell us, beginning here and ending with the last breath of Jesus (15:37). When one reflects that this passion story was penned by one whose faith was centred on a risen Lord, one must wonder at the perception of this man. A strand of tradition has made of Mark a disciple of Paul. While it is not likely that he was, literally, Paul's follower, the apostle would have found in him a kindred spirit. And one might add that the Christian church has never wholly embraced the gospel of Paul and of Mark. And understandably, for it is uncomfortable good news. To preach Christ crucified can never be comfortable or popular.

³²They went to a place called Gethsemane; and he said to his disciples, 'Sit here while I pray.' ³³He took with him **Peter and James and John**, and began to be distressed and agitated. ³⁴And said to them, 'I am deeply grieved, even to death; remain here, and keep awake,' ³⁵and going a little farther, he threw himself on the ground and prayed that, if it were possible, the hour might pass from him.

> [36]He said, Abba, Father, for you all things are possible; remove this cup from me; yet, not what I want, but what you want.' [37]He came and found them sleeping; and he said to Peter, 'Simon, are you asleep? Could you not keep awake one hour? [38]Keep awake and pray that you may not come into the time of trial; the spirit indeed is willing, but the flesh is weak.' [39]And again he went away and prayed, saying the same words. [40]And once more he came and found them sleeping, for their eyes were very heavy; and they did not know what to say to him. [41]He came a third time and said to them, 'Are you still sleeping and taking your rest? Enough! The hour has come; the Son of Man **is betrayed** into the hands of sinners. [42]Get up, let us be going. See, my **betrayer** is at hand.'

We had not long to wait for discipleship failure. All of them had heard his predictions of suffering and death; Peter, James and John had heard the heavenly voice (9:7); James and John had confidently declared their readiness to share his cup (10:38-39). Now, at Gethsemane, he took the three to be with him in his hour of need. He asked his 'disciples' to pray – they will not act as disciples. Jesus himself went apart to pray; he realised he was on his own. The presence of this inner core of disciples also serves the Marcan purpose of highlighting the significance of this passage.

Mark's Gethsemane-scene shows that Jesus did not fully understand God's way, shows that he did not want to die. While we may plausibly assert that *Abba* was Jesus' preferred address to his God, the word *abba* occurs only once in the gospels – here in Mk 14:36. There is a fittingness to its appearance here: the familiar title seems to be wrested from Jesus at this awful moment. He prayed, explicitly, that the cup be taken from him. He did not contemplate suffering and a horrible death with stoical calm. He was appalled at the prospect. He knew fear; Mark's language in vv 33-34 is very strong. Jesus was brave as he rose above his dread to embrace what his God asked. But he must know if the path which opened before him was indeed the way that God would have him walk. He found assurance in prayer: the utterance of his trustful 'Abba' already included 'Thy will be done.' His prayer did not go unanswered – though the answer was paradoxical. As the letter to the Hebrews puts it: 'He was heard because of his reverent submission' (5:7). The obedient Son cried out to the Father and put himself wholly in the hands of the Father.

If Jesus said of the disciples, 'The spirit is willing, but the flesh is weak,' that statement is not irrelevant to his own situation. Jesus himself had experienced human vulnerability: distress, agitation, and grief even to the point of death, to the point of asking the Father that the hour might pass him by and the cup be taken away. 'Hour' and 'cup' indicate the historical moment and the imminent prospect of appalling death. But this, too, was the eschatological hour of the final struggle, the great *peirasmos*, 'trial', before the triumph of God's kingdom. 'The Son of Man is given over to the hands of sinners' (v 41). In the Old Testament God gives over the wicked to punishment; here, in contrast, a just man is 'given over' by God. At the end Jesus invited his disciples: 'Get up, let us be going.' Jesus still includes his disciples, even though they had failed him.

It is important that Mark has so closely woven the theme of discipleship misunderstanding with that of Jesus' testing. It is his most dramatic answer to any objection to a suffering Messiah. Jesus himself had been brought to the brink of rejecting it. The evangelist leaves no doubt that suffering messiahship is not easily accepted; he knows, as fully as Paul, that the cross is foolishness and scandal. The three disciples did not understand. The reader is duly warned. One must watch and pray. Good intentions are not enough. Discipleship is a way of life. And the course of that way has been plotted by Jesus: 'Get up, let us be going ...'

The Arrest 14:43-52

[43]Immediately, while he was still speaking, Judas, one of the twelve, arrived; and with him there was a crowd with swords and clubs, from the chief priests, the scribes, and the elders. [44]Now **the betrayer** had given them a sign, saying, 'The one I will kiss is the man; arrest him and lead him away under guard.' [45]So when he came, he went up to him at once and said 'Rabbi!' and kissed him. [46]Then they laid hands on him and arrested him. [47]But one of those who stood near drew his sword and struck the slave of the high priest, cutting off his ear. [48]Then Jesus said to them, 'Have you come out with swords and clubs to arrest me as though I were a bandit? [49]Day after day I was with you in the temple teaching, and you did not arrest me. But let the scriptures be fulfilled.' [50]All of them deserted him and fled. [51]A certain young man was following him, wearing nothing but a linen cloth. They caught hold of him, [52]but he left the linen cloth and ran off naked.

Jesus was ready and the drama opened without delay. The Son of Man went to his fate in obedience to a divine purpose (see 14:21). His lot was indeed bitter: 'one of the twelve' was hastening to betray him. Judas was accompanied by an armed rabble, one dispatched by the religious authorities; their plot was bearing fruit (14:1-2). There is no mention of temple police (Lk 22:52) or Roman troops (Jn 18:3, 12). The 'betrayer' is, literally, 'the one who delivered him up' – Judas is serving a divine purpose. Judas greeted Jesus in the manner in which a disciple would salute his rabbi; yet betrayal with a kiss is singularly distasteful and Luke underlines the fact (Lk 22:48). In the Marcan narrative Jesus did not address Judas. The person who wounded the high priest's slave is not named; Mark gives the impression of a clumsy attempt to defend Jesus by someone other than a disciple. Jesus protested at the manner of the arrest: it characterised him as a man of violence. But he was a man of peace, a teacher who did not need to disguise his teaching. The phrase 'day by day in the temple' implies a longer Jerusalem ministry than the few days allowed by Mark. Reference to the fulfilment of the scriptures does not point to specific texts but asserts that here God's will is being done: the Son of Man is being delivered up. The 'all' who fled are the disciples. They forsook him and have forfeited the title 'disciple'. Jesus was left all alone. The mysterious young man of vv 51-52 is a parabolic figure. His shameful flight (nakedness is a symbol of nothingness and shame) dramatised disciple failure and carried its message for later disciples who may have failed. Ultimately, there is hope because of the promise of restoration (14:28: 16:7).

Before the Jewish Authorities 14:53-72

[53]They took Jesus to the high priest; and all the chief priests, the elders, and the scribes were assembled. [54]Peter had followed him at a distance, right into the courtyard of the high priest, and he was sitting with the guards, warming himself at the fire.

[55]Now the chief priests and the whole council were looking for testimony against Jesus to put him to death; but they found none. [56]For many gave false testimony against him, and **their testimony did not agree**. [57]Some stood up and gave false testimony against him, saying, [58]'We heard him say, "I will destroy this temple that is made with hands, and in three days I will build another, not made with hands".' [59]But even on this point **their testimony did not agree**. [60]Then the high priest stood up before them and asked Jesus, 'Have

you no answer? What is it that they testify against you?' 61But he was silent and did not answer. Again the high priest asked him, 'Are you the Messiah, the Son of the Blessed One?' 62Jesus said, 'I am; and 'you will see the Son of Man seated at the right hand of the Power' and 'coming with the clouds of heaven.'

63Then the high priest tore his clothes and said, 'Why do we still need witnesses?' 64You have heard his blasphemy! What is your decision?' All of them condemned him as deserving death. 65Some began to spit on him, to blindfold him, and to strike him, saying to him, 'Prophesy!' The guards also took him over and beat him.

66While Peter was below in the courtyard, one of the servant-girls of the high priest came by. 67When she saw Peter warming himself, she stared at him and said, 'You also were with Jesus, the man from Nazareth.' 68But he denied it, saying, 'I do not know or understand what you are talking about.' And he went out into the forecourt. Then the cock crowed. 69And the servant-girl, on seeing him, began again to say to the bystanders, 'This man is one of them.' 70But again he denied it. Then after a little while the bystanders again said to Peter, 'Certainly you are one of them; for you are a Galilean.' 71But he began to curse, and he swore an oath, 'I do not know the man you are talking about.' 72At that moment the cock crowed for the second time. Then Peter remembered that Jesus had said to him, 'Before the cock crows twice, you will deny me three times.' And he broke down and wept.

The opening verse (14:53) makes two affirmations: the leading away of Jesus and the assembling of priests, elders and scribes. Mark has built on the tradition that Jesus was brought before the Jewish high priest (see Lk 22:54; Jn 18:13). Peter is introduced – he had followed Jesus 'at a distance'. It will shortly emerge how very far behind he is on the way of discipleship. Jesus' testimony is framed by Peter's denials. He was faithful unto death, while Peter proved unfaithful. At Caesarea Philippi Peter showed that he could not accept the notion of suffering messiahship (8:31-33). Now he would disassociate himself from the suffering Messiah. But first the trial of Jesus got underway.

The opening remark (v 55) harks back to 3:6; 11:18; 12:12 and 14:1 – Jesus had long been tried and condemned. All that remained was how to make away with him. His enemies needed evidence. And the witnesses were there. The influence of the psalms is manifest: 'For false witnesses have risen against me, and they are breathing out violence' (Ps 27:12); 'Malicious witnesses rise up' (Ps 35:11).

Mark stresses their lack of agreement; the repetition (v 56b 'and
their testimony did not agree,' v 59, 'But even on this point their testimony did not agree') is the frame for a Marcan insertion: 'We
heard him say, "I will destroy this temple that is made with hands,
and in three days I will build another, not made with hands".' (14:
56). He thus signals the special importance of the saying.

Mark emphasises the falsity of the testimony. Yet, there is wide
attestation that Jesus had spoken against the temple (see Mt 26:61;
Jn 2:19; Acts 6:14). Besides, the cursing of the fig tree episode does
present Jesus as 'destroying the temple': 'The fig tree that you
cursed has withered' (Mk 11:21). He did claim to have brought the
temple to an end: that is the point of the mocking repetition of the
charge as he hung on the cross (15:29). Ironically, the taunt was
true, symbolically demonstrated by the rending of the temple veil
(15:38). The temple had lost its meaning for Christians. And this
was because Jesus had built another temple 'not made with hands'
– the community. This was his purpose in calling and forming disciples. John offers a different explanation: Jesus spoke of the temple
of his body (Jn 2:21).

It suits Mark's purpose that the testimony of these witnesses cannot
be the decisive factor in Jesus' trial. That must be the formal messianic claim of Jesus himself (v 62). When pressed by the high priest
to respond to the charges, Jesus maintained a rigid silence (vv 60-
61a). The silence of Jesus, carefully emphasised ('but he was silent
and did not answer,' v 61) is dramatic preparation for the solemn
confession of v 62. The high priest was forced to take direct action:
his question and Jesus' answer form the heart of this passage.
Thoroughly Marcan, these verses are the culmination of his christology. The titles 'Christ' and 'Son of God' stand in the heading of
the gospel (1:1). The high priest now ironically bestowed them on
Jesus (Son of the Blessed is the equivalent of Son of God). When
Jesus was acknowledged as Christ at Caesarea Philippi he enjoined
silence (8:30). But now Jesus himself, positively and publicly,
acknowledged that he is the Messiah, and that he is indeed Son of
God. But he did so on its own terms, in terms of 'Son of Man'. With
his firm 'I am' he made, for the first and only time, an explicit messianic claim. He could do so because now there was no risk of triumphalist misinterpretation; he was manifestly a suffering Messiah

(see 8:31). Mark's use of 'the Blessed one' and 'the Power,' though not really precise Jewish terminology, does, to his satisfaction, provide a 'Jewish' colouring. His 'you will see' refers to the Christian perception of Jesus 'at the right hand of God' by resurrection and 'coming with the clouds of heaven' at the *parousia*.

Jesus' confession provoked the death-sentence and that is how it has to be because he cannot be known for who he is until he has died and risen from the dead (see 9:9). In terms of the trial-narrative, his claim was self-incriminating. The Sanhedrin can now achieve its stated purpose (v 55). The rending of garments had become, in the case of the high priest, a carefully regulated formal judicial gesture. Only Mark (followed by Matthew) specifies a charge of blasphemy. It reflects the situation of the early church: Jewish authorities had begun to regard the Christian claims for Jesus as blasphemous. And Christians would have suffered for their confession of him (see 13:9-11). It is not unlikely, however, that Jesus, in the estimation of the Sanhedrin, was a false prophet – one who had made blasphemous claims; he had arrogated to himself divine prerogatives (such as forgiveness of sin).

Peter's denials 14:66-72

With v 66 we return to Peter. In the setting, and forms, of the denials, Mark is on traditional grounds. His title for Jesus, however, is 'Nazarene' (see 1:24; 10:47; 14:57; 16:1), indicative of his interest in Galilee. At the initial stage Peter was evasive, pretending not to understand what the maid was saying (v 68). On the basis of this first (traditional) denial Mark has built the other two, so producing his familiar triadic pattern. Peter had to come out and deny that he was 'one of them', a disciple of Jesus (v 70). Finally, he was forced to disassociate himself from Jesus, calling down the wrath of God upon himself if what he says is not true (v 71). The progression is patent: evasion, denial of discipleship, denial under oath that he had known Jesus at all. The cockcrow – Mark alone mentions that the cock crowed a second time – caused Peter to remember Jesus' prediction of his denials and his own vehement protestation (14:30-31). 'He broke down' – an approximate rendering of an enigmatic verb, but the general idea is clear enough: Peter was utterly shattered. This is the last mention of Peter in the gospel.

The denial-story brings the disciple-misunderstanding theme (promi-

nent throughout the gospel) to a head. Peter had publicly disassociated himself from Jesus. The sheep had been effectively scattered
and the stricken shepherd was wholly on his own (see 14:27). As
they see themselves in disciples who could betray and deny and
forsake, Mark's readers are not likely to feel complacent. Mark
insists on the loneliness of Jesus during his passion: up to the
moment of death he is alone, more and more alone. His intention is
not only to awaken us to the poignancy of this painful solitude. He
wants us to perceive in that starkness the truth that God alone
saves.

Before Pilate 15:1-15

[1]As soon as it was morning, the chief priests held a consultation
with the elders and scribes and the whole council. They bound
Jesus, led him away, and **handed him over** to Pilate. [2]Pilate asked
him, 'Are you the **King of the Jews**?' he answered him, 'You say so.'
[3]Then the chief priests accused him of many things. [4]Pilate asked
him again, 'Have you no answer? See how many charges they bring
against you.' [5]But Jesus made no further reply, so that Pilate was
amazed. [6]Now at the festival he used to release a prisoner for them,
anyone for whom they asked. [7]Now a man called Barabbas was in
prison with the rebels who had committed murder during the
insurrection. [8]So the crowd came and began to ask Pilate to do for
them according to his custom. [9]Then he answered them, 'Do you
want me to release for you the **King of the Jews**?' [10]For he realised
that it was out of jealousy that the chief priests had **handed him
over**. [11]But the chief priests stirred up the crowd to have him release
Barabbas for them instead. [12]Pilate spoke to them again, 'Then what
do you wish me to do with the man you call the **King of the Jews**?'
[13]They shouted back, 'Crucify him!' [14]Pilate asked them, 'Why,
what evil has he done?' but they shouted all the more, 'Crucify
him!' [15]So Pilate, wishing to satisfy the crowd, released Barabbas for
them; and after flogging Jesus, he **handed him over** to be crucified.

Mark picks up the thread of the story which had been interrupted
by the account of Peter's denials. This second meeting of the
Sanhedrin served to introduce the trial scene which followed. Jesus
was 'delivered over' to Pilate; the recurrence of this expression
throughout the passion narrative is a reminder that all is happening
'according to the definite plan and foreknowledge of God' (Acts 2:
23). It is enough to name Pilate – all Christians know who he is.

Mark has firmly presented the passion of Jesus as proclamation of
his kingship and the crucifixion as an enthronement. The theme

appears at once in Pilate's question: 'Are you the King of the Jews?' (v 2). Jesus did not reject the title out of hand but he did imply ('You say so') that he understood it differently. Pilate repeatedly calls him King of the Jews (vv 9, 12); indeed, in v 12 he is 'the man whom you (the chief priests) call the King of the Jews'. The soldiers paid homage to 'the King of the Jews' (15:16-19) and the official charge against Jesus read: 'The King of the Jews' (15:26). Priests and scribes mocked him as 'the Messiah, the King of Israel' (15:32). If, for Mark, this is a narrative of the enthronement of Christ as king, it is such in light of Jesus' profession of 14:62 – which sealed his fate (14:63-64). Jesus' royal status is wholly paradoxical. Jesus' regal authority could never resemble the authority of earthly kings (see 10:42-45).

The priests hastened to press charges against him; Jesus preserved the silence that is a feature of the suffering Just One (see Is 53:7). Pilate's 'wonder' is more than surprise; it conveys a sense of religious awe (see 5:20; Jn 19:8-11). Outside of the gospels we find no trace of the Passover amnesty described here; it would seem to be an inference drawn from this isolated Barabbas incident. Interestingly, Luke makes no mention of the custom. Barabbas was in prison with other rebels who had killed during a political affray. The crowd came to plead for this man, and Pilate presented them with an alternative: they might have instead 'the King of the Jews'. He had seen through the charges brought against Jesus. Mark puts the responsibility where he believed it belonged, at the door of the priests. As in all the gospels, Pilate was convinced of Jesus' innocence, but yielded to pressure. It is he who is really on trial; John has developed this feature in masterly fashion. Pilate's strange appeal to the crowd as to what to do with the King of the Jews is very effective. It meant that the will of the crowd would be the decisive factor. The nation rejected its king and called for his death on the cross. Pilate helplessly protested Jesus' innocence – 'Why what evil has he done?' – but they clamoured for blood. Pilate yielded, 'wishing to satisfy the crowd'. He released a murderer and condemned an innocent man. Jesus was scourged: a severe flogging was a prelude to crucifixion.

Crucifixion 15:16-32

[16]Then the soldiers led him into the courtyard of the palace (that is, the governor's headquarters); and they called together the whole cohort. [17]And they clothed him in a purple cloak; and after twisting some thorns into a crown, they put it on him. [18]And they began

saluting him, 'Hail, **King of the Jews**!' [19]They struck his head with a reed, spat upon him, and knelt down in homage to him. [20]After mocking him, they stripped him of the purple cloak and put his own clothes on him. Then they led him out to crucify him.

[21]They compelled a passer-by, who was coming in from the country, to carry his cross: it was Simon of Cyrene, the father of Alexander and Rufus. [22]Then they brought Jesus to the place called Golgatha (which means the place of a skull). [23]And they offered him wine mixed with myrrh; but he did not take it. [24]nd they crucified him, and divided his clothes among them, casting lots to decide what each should take.

[25]It was nine o'clock in the morning when they crucified him. [26]The inscription of the charge against him read, '**The King of the Jews**.' [27]And with him they crucified two bandits, one on his right and one on his left. [29]Those who passed by derided him, shaking their heads and saying, 'Aha! You who would destroy the temple and build it in three days, [30]save yourself, and come down from the cross!' [31]In the same way, the chief priests, along with the scribes, were also mocking him among themselves and saying, 'He saved others; he cannot save himself. [32]Let the Messiah, the **King of Israel**, come down from the cross now, so that we may see and believe.' Those who were crucified with him also taunted him.

Death by crucifixion was, and was intended to be, degrading. Even the choice of the place of Jesus' execution was a calculated insult. Archaeological research has shown that Golgatha, a disused quarry, was, at that time, a refuse-dump. There was nothing of majesty about the death of Jesus, no trace of glory.

The Marcan drama reached its climax in the crucifixion scene. The evangelist had warned of Jesus' death in 3:6; from that point on, explicitly or by allusion, he continued to harp on it. In painting this scene he has drawn upon Old Testament passages portraying the figure of the suffering Just One, who suffers but is finally vindicated. Various motifs which build up the image of the Just One, taken mainly from the psalms, surface in this passage. Mark's concern is to establish that everything took place according to the scriptures, that is, according to the will of God.

It was customary for the condemned man to carry his cross beam. Mark tells us that a certain Simon of Cyrene (a town in North Africa, but perhaps Simon now lived in Palestine) was 'impressed' by the soldiers to carry the beam. Alexander and Rufus were evidently known to Mark's community. Golgatha, an Aramaic name, means 'a skull'. The name may have been suggested by a skull-shaped hill, though the text speaks only of 'place' and does not specify hill. It was presumably outside the city wall and close to a road (v 29). It was Jewish custom, based on Proverbs 31:6-7, to provide condemned criminals with drugged wine as a means of lessening their torment. Jesus, in Gethsemane, had accepted the Father's will, and accepted it wholeheartedly; he will not take the wine. And they crucified him – no more simply could the dread act be recorded. By custom, the clothes of the condemned fell to the executioners. Mark, with Ps 22:18 in mind, saw in this, too, a divine purpose.

The evangelist marks the time off in three-hourly intervals (15:25, 33, 34). For that matter, precise statements of time are a feature of the trial and passion narrative: 14:72; 15:1, 25, 33, 42; 16;1. This is to indicate that the passage of time was in accord with the will of God. Nothing at all has happened by chance or unexpectedly. The third hour is 9am. It is impossible to reconcile this time reference with John 19:14 where Jesus was sentenced at 12 noon of 14 Nisan. John's purpose is to have Jesus die at the hour when the Passover lambs were slaughtered. Both evangelists are making theological statements.

The superscription (15:26) is in accordance with Roman practice; for Mark it indicates that the King is now enthroned. All the gospels agree that Jesus was crucified between two criminals. Many manuscripts of Mark carry as v 28: 'And the scripture was fulfilled which says, "He was reckoned with the transgressors".' It is a borrowing from Lk 22:37, but it does make explicit the intent of Mark who would have seen in this disturbing fact a fulfilment of Is 13:12. Jesus who, at the arrest, had protested that he was no bandit, now is crucified between bandits. Two sets of taunts were levelled at Jesus. The fact that there were passersby suggests crucifixion near a roadway. Their taunt was influenced by Lamentations 2:15 and Ps 22:7-8 – 'They wag their heads'; 'He committed his cause to the Lord; let him deliver him, let him rescue him.' And they 'derided', literally 'blasphemed' him. They were, of course, really blaspheming God, so doing the very thing that justified Jesus' condemnation to death (14:64). Their words harked back to the temple charge in 14:58. The irony is that precisely by not saving his life (8:35), by not coming down from the cross, Jesus was bringing the temple to an end (15: 38) and building the new temple.

The mocking invitation for Jesus to come down from the cross was echoed by the leaders of official Judaism. The presence of the chief priests at the crucifixion and their cruel railing cannot be historical. But, in Mark's storyline it is fitting that they should be the principal scoffers. They, implacable opponents of Jesus, had to be fitted in at this climactic moment. 'He saved others' – a reference to Jesus' ministry of healing, regularly described as *sózein*, 'to heal' or 'to save' (e.g. 5:23, 28, 34). It is in his death that Jesus accomplished salvation and was perceived to be the Son of God. This becomes clear in the episode of 15:27-39. Here, Jesus was three times challenged – by the passersby (vv 29-30), by the religious leaders (vv 31-32a) and by those crucified with him (15:32b) – to come down from the cross and thereby save himself. Jesus would not rise to the challenge. As one who had warned the disciples, 'Those who want to save their life will lose it' (8:25), and as the Son who wills what the Father wills (14:36), Jesus makes no attempt to save his life. Mark is making a theological point: salvation is never of oneself, not even for Jesus. Nor is there any hope of salvation from an Elijah-figure (vv 35-36).

Up to now Jesus had been 'King of the Jews'; now he is 'the Messiah, the King of Israel'. Since Maccabean times 'Jews' had become the Gentile name for the people of Israel, so 'King of the Jews' is normal with Pilate; the priests, naturally, used 'Israel' as a self-designation. Jewish tradition had anticipated that in the days of Messiah the true Israel would be established. Now Jesus is being ironically addressed as King of this eschatological Israel. They are still looking for 'signs' (see 8:11-12): if Jesus does come down from the cross they will 'see' and believe. In Mark 'seeing' is primarily associated with the 'seeing' of Jesus at the *parousia* (13:26; 14:62). But there can be no 'seeing' until Jesus has died and risen. Temple sayings and christological titles, prominent in 14:58 and 14:51-62, are brought together here (15:29, 32); the significance of both is being worked out on the cross. The denouement comes in 15:38-39. Meanwhile, Jesus' isolation is total: even his companions in suffering derided him (v 32b).

Death and Revelation 15:33-41
33When it was noon, darkness came over the whole land until three in the afternoon. 34At three o'clock Jesus cried out **with a loud voice, 'Eloi, Eloi, lema sabachtani?'** which means, 'My God, my God, why have you forsaken me?' 35When some of the listeners heard it, they

said, 'Listen, he is calling for Elijah.' [36]And someone ran, filled a
sponge with sour wine, put it on a stick, and gave it to him to drink,
saying, 'Wait, let us see whether Elijah will come to take him down.'
[37]Then Jesus gave **a loud cry** and breathed his last. [38]And the curtain of the temple was torn in two, from top to bottom.
[39]Now when the centurion, who stood facing him, saw that in this
way he breathed his last, he said, '**Truly this man was God's Son!**'
[40]There were also women looking on from a distance; among them
were Mary Magdalene, and Mary the mother of James the younger
and of Joses, and Salome. [41]These used to follow him and provided
for him when he was in Galilee; and there were many other women
who had come up with him to Jerusalem.

The grim drama was being played out. Crucified at the third hour
(9am), Jesus had spent three hours in agony. Now, at the sixth hour
(noon), broke the hour of darkness, of momentary demonic triumph – 'your hour, and the power of darkness' (Lk 2:53); see Amos
8:9-10). Jesus had begun his mission in an encounter with Satan (Mk
1:12-13) and carried on the war in his exorcisms. Now, helpless on
the cross, he seemed to be crushed by these very powers. The close
of that time of darkness, the ninth hour (3pm), marked the hour of
fulfilment. Paradoxically, it seemed to sound the nadir of Jesus'
defeat. This is brought out by the twofold reference to a 'loud cry'.
The expression *phóné megalé* occurs only four times in Mark. In 1:26
and 5:7 it is the loud cry of a demoniac, one oppressed by an evil
spirit. Jesus himself now (vv 34, 37) reacted with a loud cry to the
intolerable pressure of evil. He suffered the absence of God: his cry
of dereliction was one of total desolation: 'My God, my God, why
have you forsaken me?' His words are the opening of Psalm 22 – a
lament. Lament is the cry of a suffering righteous person addressed
to the One who can bring an end to suffering. Mark has Jesus die in
total isolation, without any relieving feature at all. It would have
seemed that, up to this point, Jesus' isolation could go no further:
deserted by his disciples, taunted by his enemies, derided by those
who hung with him, suffocating in the darkness of evil. But the
worst was now: abandoned by God. His suffering was radically
lonely. But his God was 'my God' (v 34). Even in this, as at
Gethsemane, it was 'not what I want, but what you want'. Here,
even more than then, the sheer humanness of Jesus was manifest.
And his experience was a thoroughly human one. It underlines the
difference between feeling and reality. The feeling: one of

Godforsakenness. The reality: never were Father and Son more at one. It is akin to the experience of Job who also suffered the absence of God; or of later mystics, suffering the 'dark night of the soul'. God had never withdrawn; the feeling is that he had.

The bystanders thought that Jesus called on Elijah (v 35), who was popularly believed to come to the aid of the just in tribulation. Misunderstanding hounded Jesus to the end. 'Sour wine' is the Roman soldiers' *posca* – a cheap red wine. The gesture was kindly meant (v 36), but Mark, likely with Ps 69:21 in mind – 'They gave me gall for food, and for my thirst they gave me vinegar to drink' – thinks of it as an addition to Jesus' misery. Again the 'loud cry' is significant: it depicts awareness of his struggle with evil. All the more so because Mark describes a sudden, violent death – 'breathed his last' is not strong enough to convey its meaning (v 37). Jesus died abandoned, seemingly crushed by the forces of evil. This is perfectly in keeping with Mark's *theologia crucis*. Forthwith, he can point to the victory of Jesus.

At the end of the passage, vv 27-39, Mark focuses on the theme of Jesus as 'the Son of God'. In contrast to the mocking challenges hurled at the dying Jesus (15:29-32), there is an emphatically positive response to Jesus' death. The centurion in charge of the execution stood facing a helpless victim on a cross and watched him as he died. He declared, in awe: 'Truly, this man was God's Son!' (v 39). His declaration is to be viewed in the context of the rending of the temple curtain from top to bottom (v 38). The temple had lost its significance (see 11:12-25; 13:2; 14:58). It was the end of the cult through which God had hitherto mediated forgiveness of sin and salvation. Mark's theological point is that a Jesus who had known the pang of Godforsakenness was now wholly vindicated. The temple curtain 'was torn' – by God! Salvation is henceforth mediated uniquely through the shedding of his blood by the wholly faithful Son of God. Jesus had already proclaimed as much. He had done so in his words to his disciples: 'For the Son of Man came not to be served but to serve, and to give his life a ransom for many [all]' (10:45). And in his words at the farewell supper: 'This is my blood of the covenant which is poured out for many [all]' (14:24). The temple is gone. God's Son is henceforth the 'place' of salvation. 'Truly this man was God's Son.' The chief priests had demanded, in mockery,

'Let the Messiah, the King of Israel, come down from the cross now, so that we may see and believe' (v 32). Now, a Gentile saw and believed. His is a profession of Christian faith. It is the clincher to Mark's theological stance that the revelation of God's Son took place on the cross.

The Twelve had fled. Yet, Jesus had not been wholly deserted – a little group of women disciples remained (vv 40-44). Mark says of them: 'They used to follow him and provided for him when he was in Galilee; and there were many other women who had come up with him to Jerusalem' (15:41). The women had 'followed him' – *akolouthein* is a technical term for discipleship. And they had 'served' Jesus: they are authentic disciples. Although this is the only place in the gospel where the discipleship of women is mentioned in explicit terms, we should not overlook the reference to 'many other women'. We must recognise that throughout the gospel 'disciple' is an inclusive term. It is because they had continued to follow him if only 'at a distance' (v 40) – as women they could not be at the very place of execution – that the final message is entrusted to them (16:1-8).

The Burial 15:42-47

42When evening had come, and since it was the day of Preparation, that is, the day before the Sabbath, 43Joseph of Arimathea, a respected member of the council, who was also himself waiting expectantly for the kingdom of God, went boldly to Pilate and asked for the body of Jesus. 44Then Pilate wondered if he were already dead; and, summoning the centurion, he asked him whether he had been dead for some time. 45When he learned from the centurion that he was dead, he granted the body to Joseph. 46Then Joseph bought a linen cloth, and taking down the body, wrapped it in the linen cloth, and laid it in a tomb that had been hewn out of the rock. He then rolled a stone against the door of the tomb. 47Mary Magdalene and Mary the mother of Joses saw where the body was laid.

The story of Jesus' burial was important because it established that Jesus had really died and because it assured that the women had seen where the body had been placed. This was crucial in view of the manner of the burial. Mark sticks to his three-hour scheme even though the 'evening' (6pm) would mean that the Sabbath had begun. The 'day of preparation' (v 42) – here is where we learn that Jesus died on a Friday. The disciples had fled at the arrest of Jesus

(14:50). It was left to another to bury him. Joseph of Arimathea, a Sanhedrin member and Torah-observant, was concerned to fulfil the law – here, that the body of one crucified should not be left overnight on the tree (Deut 21:23).

In Roman eyes Jesus was a duly executed criminal; disposal of the body was the business of the Roman authorities. Joseph approached Pilate and was duly granted the corpse of Jesus (vv 42-46). It would be a hasty, dishonourable burial of one executed on a charge of blasphemy – as the sanhedrist Joseph would have assessed it. The body was not anointed. It was simply wrapped in a linen shroud and placed in a niche of that disused quarry. A far cry, indeed, from the royal burial of the fourth gospel (Jn 19:38-42). We need to be sensitive to the theological concerns of the evangelists. The only witnesses of the burial were women, a preparation for the final passage of the gospel (16:1-8).

The Epilogue 16:1-8
   [1]When the Sabbath was over, Mary Magdalene, and Mary the mother of James, and Salome bought spices, so that they might go and anoint him. [2]And very early on the first day of the week, when the sun had risen, they went to the tomb. [3]They had been saying to one another, 'Who will roll away the stone for us from the entrance to the tomb?' [4]When they looked up, they saw that the stone, which was very large, had already been rolled back. [5]As they entered the tomb, they saw a young man, dressed in a white robe, sitting on the right side; and they were alarmed. [6]But he said to them, 'Do not be alarmed; you are looking for Jesus of Nazareth, who was crucified. He has been raised; he is not here. Look, there is the place where they laid him. [7]But go, tell his disciples and Peter that he is going ahead of you to Galilee: there you will see him, just as he told you.' [8]So they went out and fled from the tomb, for terror and amazement had seized them; and **they said nothing to anyone, for they were afraid.**

Mark relates that the three women named in 15:40, intending to anoint the body of Jesus, bought spices when the sabbath had ended (after 6pm). Their purpose is in step with the hasty burial (15: 46). The large stone that sheltered the body would have presented a problem. To their surprise, they found that the stone 'had already been rolled back'. This is the divine passive: God had acted!

The 'young man', dressed in white, is an angel. Their awe and his words of assurance are stock features of such angelic visitations.

They had come seeking Jesus; they had seen where his body had been laid (15:47). Again they look upon the spot, but he is no longer there. The 'young man' plays the role of *angelus interpres*, of inter-preting angel, a feature of apocalyptic. They were faced with the riddle of an empty tomb: he explains why the tomb is empty. It is a neat literary way of presenting, as briefly as possible, the fact of the empty tomb and the real reason of its emptiness. This 'young man', besides, recalls the *neaniskos* in 14:51-52. That 'young man' repres-ented, parabolically, the failure of disciples; here the disciples are, vaguely, in the background.

The women had sought Jesus of Nazareth: an important title for Mark. He has used it from the beginning (1:9, 24) and stresses it again at the end (14:67; 16:6), a reminder that Jesus is the man of Galilee. And he is 'the crucified one'– practically a title also. 'He has been raised': the answer to the cry of Godforsakenness (15:34). Jesus has not been forsaken! Apparent failure has been transformed into victory – by God.

The women were given a message, the echo of a promise made by Jesus on the way to Gethsemane (14:28), a message for the disciples, and especially for Peter (that is the force of the Greek). Jesus is going before them into Galilee; they will see him there. Galilee is a symbol as much as a place. Mark has been at pains to show the wider 'Galilee' as the place of the breakdown of the barrier between Jew and Gentile, as the locale of the Gentile mission. There the disci-ples had been first assembled (1:16-20) and there they will now 'see': they will encounter the Risen Christ. And there, too, they will 'see' the Son of Man at his coming (13:26-27; 14:62). Meanwhile, life goes on in the darkness of faith, for Jesus is not yet fully revealed. The cross still casts its shadow and life is real and earnest (13:9-13). But the consummation is sure and will be as fully a reality as the former ministry in Galilee.

The men disciples of Jesus had abandoned him and fled for their lives (14:50). The women disciples did not lose heart: they followed him as far as women might, looking on the crucifixion-scene 'from afar' (15:40). Mark names three of the group – the impression is of a relatively large group. They were Galileans who had 'followed' Jesus and had 'come up with him' to Jerusalem – again discipleship. It is because they had continued to follow him, if even 'from afar', that the Easter message is entrusted to them. They alone, of all others, had followed to the cross. The chosen men disciples had abandoned Jesus. These women disciples have stood steadfast and have not been ashamed of Jesus (8:38).

But have not the women, too, failed at the end? They were given a message: 'Go, tell his disciples and Peter that he is going ahead of you to Galilee' (16:7). But what kind of messengers did they turn out to be? – 'They said nothing to anyone, for they were afraid (*ephobounto gar*)' (v 8). They, too, experienced the basic ground of discipleship failure: fear.

The other evangelists agree in asserting that the women did, in fact, fulfil their messenger role: Mt 28:6-10; Lk 24:4-11; Jn 20:17-18. Evidently, a well-established tradition. Mark, then, has, consciously, painted a different picture. Why? Francis Moloney provides a satisfying answer:

> Mark 16:1-8 is the masterstroke of a storyteller who, up to this point, has relentlessly pursued the steady movement towards failure of all the male disciples. The evidence of the tradition (seen in the gospels of Matthew, Luke, and John) indicates that women were the first witnesses of the Easter event, and reported an Easter message to the unbelieving and discouraged disciples. This was well known by members of early Christian communities. In this, Matthew, Luke, and John, each in their own way, are closer to what happened on that Sunday morning. But Mark has changed the story. Why has Mark taken a well-known tradition and altered it so radically? There is something profoundly Pauline in what Mark is trying to do as he takes away all initiative from human beings and places it with God. As with the promises of Jesus' forthcoming death and resurrection (8:31; 9:31; 10:33-34), the promises of 14:28 and 16:7 will be fulfilled. What Jesus said would happen, will happen … The reader has every reason to believe that the promises of 14:28 and 16:7 have already come true. But Jesus' meeting with the disciples and Peter in Galilee does not take place within the limitations of the story. It cannot, because the women do not obey the word of the young man. They, like the disciples, fail; they flee in fear (16:8).
>
> When and how does Jesus' meeting with the failed disciples, women and men, take place? The answer to that question cannot

be found in the story; but the very existence of the story tells the reader that what Jesus said would happen did happen. The gospel of Mark, with its faith-filled prologue telling of God's design for the human situation in the gift of his Son (1:1-13) addresses a believing community. This indicates that the disciples and Peter did see Jesus in Galilee as he had promised... There is no record of any such encounter within the narrative. It is not required, as the believing community has the word itself: 'Jesus has been raised' (16:6). If the promise of 14:28 and 16:7 had been thwarted, there would be no Christian community, and thus no gospel of Mark, read and heard within the community. 'This is the end of Mark's story, because it is the beginning of discipleship.' (*The Gospel of Mark*, Hendrickson, 2002, 350-352).

In the end all human beings fail. God alone succeeds. The Father had not abandoned the Son (15:34) but had raised Jesus from the dead (16:6). The failed disciples will encounter the risen Lord in Galilee, not because they have succeeded, but solely because of the initiative of God. The account of a reunion with the Risen One promised in 14:28 and again in 16:7 is not in the text of Mark's gospel. The Lord will be encountered in the Christian community that received the story.

The Appendix 16:9-20

If, today, we acknowledge that Mark did intend to end his gospel at 16: 8, this was not always so. Even early Christians had been disconcerted by this abrupt closure of the gospel. A second century author decided to round off Mark's work – in our 16:9-20. Though rather widely attested, the fact remains that in the older Greek manuscripts of Mark and in important manuscripts of early versions, this passage does not appear. The vocabulary and style of the passage show that it was not written by Mark; it is based on a knowledge of the traditions found in the other gospels and Acts.

> [9]Now after he rose early on the first day of the week, he appeared first to Mary Magdalene, from whom he had cast out seven demons. [10]She went out and told those who had been with him, while they were mourning and weeping, [11]but when they heard that he was alive and had been seen by her, they would not believe it.
>
> [12]After this he appeared in another form to two of them, as they were walking into the country. [13]And they went back and told the rest, but they did not believe them.
>
> [14]Later he appeared to the eleven themselves as they were sitting at the table; and he upraided them for their lack of faith and stubbornness, because they had not believed those who saw him after he had risen. [15]And he said to them, 'Go into all the world and proclaim the good news to the whole creation. [16]The one who believes and is baptised will be saved; but the one who does not believe will be condemned. [17]And these signs will accompany those who believe: by using my name they will cast out demons; they will speak in new tongues; [18]they will pick up snakes in their hands, and if they drink any deadly thing, it will not hurt them; they will lay their hands on the sick, and they will recover.'
>
> [19]So then the Lord Jesus, after he had spoken to them, was taken up into heaven and sat down at the right hand of God. [20]And they went out and proclaimed the good news everywhere, while the Lord worked with them and confirmed the message by the signs that accompanied it.

No serious attempt has been made to knit this ending closely with

the Marcan text. Thus, v 9 looks back, not to 16:8 but to 16:2. Mary
Magdalene is introduced as though she had not been named in 15:
40; 16:1. The four main sections are loosely linked:

The appearance to Mary Magdalene 16:9-11
These verses owe much to Jn 20:11-18 and Lk 24:10-11. The description of Mary as she 'from whom he had cast out seven demons'
comes from Lk 8:2.

The appearance to two travellers 16:12-13
No more than an echo of the Emmaus narrative, Lk 24: 13-35.

The appearance to the eleven 16:14-18
See Lk 24:36-49; Jn 20:19-23; Mt 28:18-20. The reproach (v 14) is
severe, more so than in 8:14-21. The writer stresses, for his day, the
vital importance of the resurrection of Jesus, its basic place in
Christian faith. The commission to preach the gospel (vv 15-16)
may be based on Mt 28:18-19, or may be a parallel version of a saying which emerged in a Gentile church. The signs of vv 17-18 are
those recorded in the synoptics and Acts. See Mk 3:15; Acts 2:3-4;
10:46; 19:6; Lk 10:19; Acts 28:3-4; Mk 6:13.

Ascension and apostolic mission 16:19-20
See Lk 24:50-53; Acts 1:4-14. The ascension of the 'Lord Jesus' – a
title frequent in Acts but found nowhere else in the gospels – is
described in words borrowed from the story of Elijah (2 Kgs 2:11)
and from Ps 110:1. Verse 20 obviously presupposes a period of missionary activity. The Lord Jesus himself co-operates with his minis-
ters in their preaching of the gospel.

The author of the Ending did achieve his purpose. He resolved the
enigmatic ending of 16:8, continued the gospel themes of discipleship failure and mission and filled out the brief reference to resurrection in 16:6 with appearances of the risen Jesus. Yet he has blunted
the stark message of Mark. The verdict stands: 'The author has
betrayed one of the fundamental purposes of Mark, the original
evangelist, whose version of the story of Jesus closed with the fear,
flight, and silence of the women in 16:8. Rather than ask the readers
of the gospel to 'fill the gap' left by the failure of the women in 16:8,
especially by means of the promises of Jesus in 14:27 and 16:7, he
provides all the 'filling' that second-century readers might have
wanted … It catches only part of what Mark wished to say to the

church by ending the cospel at 16:8. The flight and silence of the women force readers to ask where they stand, relying only upon the action of God to make divine sense of human nonsense. This message is challenging, and not particularly comforting in the light of our repeatedly failing attempts to determine our own future and God's ways within that future.' (F. J. Moloney, *The Gospel of Mark*, 362).

Glossary

I hope that reference to this glossary will spare the reader the chore of searching out in the text the meaning of some recurring terms.

Allegory – Allegory (where the details of a story have symbolic value as in the Wicked Tenants [Mk 12:1-8]) is extended metaphor and, as such, is a story that has both a literal and a metaphorical level. An allegorical story can well be a parable – as in the example cited. There are several allegorical parables in the gospels.

Apocalyptic – 'Apocalypse', from the Greek *apocalypsis*, ('revelation') designates a type of Jewish literature which flourished from about 200BC to 100AD. As a literary form it is presented as a revelation, or series of revelations, of heavenly secrets made to a seer and conveyed in highly symbolic imagery. It is a crisis literature. The biblical apocalypses are the book of Daniel (more precisely, Dan 7-12) and the Revelation of John. Apocalypticism is the worldview of an apocalyptic movement. In this view it is taken for granted that a supernatural world stands above our earthly world. That heavenly world is the 'real' world. There is a twofold dualism: vertical, the world above and our world, and horizontal, our age and the age to come. There is always a definitive eschatological judgement: the final clash between good and evil, issuing in the total victory of God and the end of evil. Apocalyptic ideas pervade the New Testament.

Apostle – The Christian mission was carried out by 'apostles' – those 'sent out' (*apostellein*) from the Christian communities. The passage Acts 13:1-4, the designation and sending out by the Antioch community of Barnabas and Saul, is an eloquent instance of this. There has been an unfortunate confusion of 'Twelve' and 'apostle.' The Twelve were 'apostles' in the sense that they had been 'sent out' by Jesus. 'Apostle' has a much wider range than the Twelve.

Christology – In Jesus of Nazareth, God is really and truly present. That is the great Christian truth. But to seek to define the mysterious nature of Jesus is a precarious endeavour. Not alone have such attempts been made but, for centuries, it has been assumed that the fifth-century council of Chalcedon had spoken the definitive christological word – all that remained was commentary. Christology (theological understanding of Jesus) became, in practice, a subtle word-game around the formula of Chalcedon. The question to be answered at Chalcedon was whether God's salvation had been given, once for all, in the man Jesus. Because the answer had to be Yes, and because salvation is of God, it had to be asserted, in the theological language of the day, that God himself was present in the man Jesus. That had been said, long before, by Paul: 'God was in Christ, reconciling the world to himself' (2 Cor 11:25). In this sense, too, one understands the christology of Mark.

Covenant – Originally a treaty graciously 'granted' by an overlord. God gave a covenant to his people at Sinai ('I am your God; you are my people') sealed and ratified in the blood of a sacrificial victim. Jeremiah spoke of a 'new covenant' (Jer 31:31-34). This new covenant with the new people of God was given through Jesus and sealed in his blood (see 1 Cor 11:25).

Disciple – Jesus gathered around himself a group of committed disciples, some of whom were also active in the early church. Distinctive features of this initial discipleship were: Jesus took the initiative in calling; 'following' meant literal, physical following of an itinerant preacher; disciples were warned that they might face suffering and hostility. The evidence is clear that some women did follow Jesus during his ministry in Galilee and accompanied him on his last journey to Jerusalem (see Mk 15:40-41). 'Disciple' is an inclusive term.

Eschatological – Pertaining to the **eschaton**, the End. Eschatology refers to the new age, the transformation of our world. But, with the coming of Jesus, this new age has already begun – we await the consummation. In the preaching of Jesus the kingdom of God is eschatological: the definitive intervention of God, his kingly reign, is (in Jesus) a present reality. It seems that Jesus thought of himself as the eschatological prophet.

Kerygma – The 'heralding' or 'preaching' of the good news: the missionary preaching of the good news to Jews and Gentiles.

Kingdom of God – The precise phrase 'kingdom of God' occurs only once in the Old Testament, in Wisdom 10:10. The expression was not current in Judaism at the time of Jesus and was not widely

used by early Christians. 'Kingdom of God' is found predominant-
ly in the synoptics and then almost always on the lips of Jesus. It
was evidently central to Jesus' proclamation. Israel regarded God
as universal King. And there was the expectation that God's reign
would soon be manifested over the whole world. This is why
'reign' or 'rule' of God is a more satisfactory rendering of the
Aramaic *malkutha di' elaha*. 'Kingdom of God' is, however, tradi-
tionally firmly in place. Jesus spoke, in the main, of a future kingdom: God will reveal himself in power and glory. There is evidence
that Jesus also spoke of the kingdom as in some sort already present
in his own words and deeds. When we have in mind the fact that
the kingdom of God is not primarily a state or place, but rather the
dynamic event of God coming in power to rule his people Israel in
the end-time, it is not surprising that the precise relationship
between the future and present kingdom is not specified. That is
why Jesus can speak of the kingdom as both imminent and yet present. In Jesus' eyes his healings and exorcisms were part of the
eschatological drama that was already underway and that God was
about to bring to its conclusion. The important point is that Jesus
deliberately chose to proclaim that the display of miraculous power
throughout his ministry was a preliminary and partial realisation of
God's kingly rule.

Messiah – From a Hebrew word meaning 'anointed'. In Greek it is
rendered *christos*, whence 'Christ'. In Jewish expectation the
Messiah would be God's instrument (not a divine figure) in usher-
ing in his kingdom. The expectation is a development of the promise
to David in 2 Samuel 7:11-16 – expectation of a royal Messiah. In the
New Testament, Jesus is 'son of David'. It is unlikely that Jesus himself ever claimed to be the Messiah. It is also very likely that Jesus'
opponents may have understood him and his followers to claim
that he was the Messiah. After the resurrection, of course, Jesus
was, by his followers, regularly called the Messiah – Jesus Christ
(Messiah). But he was a paradoxical Messiah: one who suffered and
died on a cross – not the triumphalist royal messiah of popular
expectation.

Messianic Secret – It was firmly Mark's view that no human being
could acknowledge in faith and truth that Jesus is the Son of God
before the paradoxical revelation of his identity through his death

on the cross. Throughout Mark's gospel we find Jesus repeatedly imposing silence in reference to his identity or role. This is Mark's 'Messianic Secret'. It really is a misnomer. The element of secrecy concerns not Jesus' messiahship but his identity as Son of God. This was recognised and professed by the centurion at the cross (15:39).

Parable – A parable is a brief story with two levels of meaning. For instance, at first sight, the Sower looks like an agricultural vignette. Its true meaning has to do with reception of the gospel message. Always the second level of meaning is the essential one. The purpose of a parable is to challenge decision and invite action.

Parousia – The Greek word *parousia* means 'presence' or 'arrival'. It was, in the ancient Greek-speaking world, used of the ceremonial visit of a ruler or of the apparition of a god. In the New Testament it is used of the 'appearance' or coming of the glorified Christ at the close of salvation history. It expresses, in dramatic fashion, faith in a final act of God marking the goal of human history, and the establishment, in its fullness, of the kingdom of God. After New Testament times this came to be known, somewhat unhelpfully, as the Second Coming of Christ. The earliest Christians expected this consummation in their own time. And the expectation may be, and is, often present without use of the term *parousia*.

In practice, *parousia* is one of the more abstruse themes of New Testament study. Firstly, there is the concept itself. Then there is the prevalence of expectation of a proximate *parousia*, with, however, warnings that the precise time of its occurrence was entirely unknown. *Parousia* has to be viewed against an apocalyptic background. A feature of apocalyptic is keen expectation of the End: it was thought that God's final intervention would follow hard on a perceived historical crisis. There is a looking to life beyond death, a life very different from the life of our experience. There is always a definitive judgement. There will be triumphant vindication of the elect. All of this lies behind the imagery of the Son of Man coming in glory.

The New Testament presents a message that is linked to a salvation history which had a beginning, which developed, and which was oriented to an end fixed from the start, an end which would be marked by the triumph of God and of humanity over all forces of evil. Yet, certain as is the end of the world, it is not at all easy to represent it. This could only be done in imaginative and symbolic language. Besides, Christians soon experienced the delay of the expected *parousia*. It was perceived that the nearness of the end was not a question of date but a theological affirmation. The incarnation, resurrection and exaltation of Jesus Christ have brought the religious history of humankind nearly to the goal of its term. This is the last age – no matter how long it may endure.

Perhaps it is best to recognise that *parousia* is myth. Myth is a symbolic form of expression couched in narrative that is not intended to be historical. It deals with realities that transcend experience. The *parousia* is just such a reality: the final victory of God in Christ made wholly manifest. This can only be expressed in symbol and imagery. It is, properly understood, myth.

Pharisees – The Pharisees seem to have had their origin in a religious and political response to the policy of Hellenisation launched by Antiochus IV (175-163BC), king of the Seleucid kingdom which included Palestine, and his Jewish supporters. In furthering his policy of imposing Greek cultural and religious practices, he launched an official persecution of the Jewish religion and profaned the Temple by setting up an altar to Zeus. The Pharisees formed a religious and political grouping of devout Jews who perceived a threat to the very existence of Jews as a distinct ethnic, cultural and religious entity. They emphasised detailed study and observance of the Law of Moses. Besides, they also possessed a normative body of tradition – the traditions of the 'fathers' or 'elders'. While they acknowledged that some of these legal rules and practices went beyond the Law, they maintained that such practices were, nevertheless, God's will for Israel. They actively engaged in trying to convince ordinary Jews to observe these Pharisaic practices in their daily life. Much of what is attributed to Pharisaic teaching refers to legal rulings or opinions regarding concrete behaviour (*halakoth*) in matters of purity rules, sabbath observance, tithing, marriage and divorce. The Pharisees lacked political power but would have had some political influence. As a major religious force, they enjoyed the respect of the people. After 70AD and the destruction of the Jerusalem Temple by the Romans, as practically the only religious group to have survived the Jewish War, their influence would have increased.

All four gospels attest to frequent contact of Jesus with Pharisees throughout his ministry. This relationship was, not surprisingly, one of tension because he and they addressed the same constituency. He and they sought to influence the main body of Palestinian Jews and win them to their respective visions of what God was calling Israel to be. Jesus would have challenged them directly and in parable. In prophetic mode, he may have pronounced woes against them. Yet the gospels acknowledge that some Pharisees were willing to give Jesus a serious hearing (e.g. Lk 7:36–50; Jn 3:1-2). Their relationship would have been notably less hostile than that represented in Mt 23. It is noteworthy that Pharisees are practically absent in all gospel passion narratives. The death of Jesus was brought about, historically, not by Pharisees, but by a religious and political alliance of Jerusalem priesthood and Roman political authority.

Scribes – The emergence of writing is the obvious starting point for scribes. The word 'scribe' in Hebrew, Greek and other languages had a wide range of meaning, open to change over time and open to a variety of social roles. Scribes functioned in the ancient Near East over millennia. They wrote, copied and guarded records for tax and military purposes, annals for government archives, and religious texts. Palestinian scribes in Jesus' time were, in fact, bureaucrats. In Jerusalem they assisted the priests in judicial and religious proceedings in the Sanhedrin. They would have played a secretarial role and, as in a modern civil service, some might have had a measure of influence. On the whole, they were 'retainers'. The gospels seem to suggest that the scribes, as a homogenous group, formed part of a united front against Jesus. This is unhistorical.

Sadducees – Information on the Sadducees is meagre. The name likely comes from Zadok, the priest of David and Solomon. In short, the Sadducees were a small group of priestly and lay aristocrats based in Jerusalem. They were theologically conservative, sticking to the clear teaching of the Torah (Pentateuch). See Acts 26:6-10. The Sadducees appear rarely in the synoptics – once only in Mark (12: 18-27) and are completely absent from John and Paul.

Son of God – The New Testament church confessed Jesus as Son of God – and, in doing so, attributed to Jesus a unique relationship to God. The question, then, is: was the title Son of God bestowed on Jesus during his lifetime? The title was used, in association with

Messiah, by the high priest (Mk 14:61) – but the exchange between the high priest and Jesus (14:61–62) reflects the christology of the evangelist. The heavenly voice, at baptism and transfiguration, declaring Jesus to be 'my Son, the Beloved' (1:11; 9:7) is for the sake of the reader. The confession of the centurion (15:39), at that moment in the gospel, is a firm christological statement. Ironically, the one text in which Jesus referred to himself absolutely as the Son ('about that day or hour no one knows, neither the angels in heaven, nor the Son, but only the father,' 13:32) implies his subordination to the Father. On the other hand, Jesus did address God in Aramaic as *Abba* (14:36). There is no evidence that, in Palestinian Judaism, *abba* was used in address to God. Jesus' usage is distinctive and suggests his consciousness of a unique relationship. As for the meaning of 'Son of God' – the voice from heaven is a composite quotation: from Ps 2:7; Is 42:1; Gen 22:2. In Is 42:1 the servant in whom God delights is one 'chosen' for ministry; in Gen 22:2 Abraham's beloved son is his 'only' son. Most importantly, in Ps 2:7, 'you are my son' is declared by the Lord of the Davidic king. Consequently, God solemnly affirms that Jesus, the Anointed one from the line of David, is his only or unique Son whom he has chosen for eschatological ministry. Jesus did not refer to himself, directly, as Son of God.

Son of Man – 'The Son of Man' occurs more than eighty times in the gospels and, practically without exception, as a self-designation by Jesus. He, however, never set out the meaning of the phrase; nor was it ever used to identify him. The expression itself is a literal rendering of the Aramaic idiom *bar 'enasha*, meaning 'man'. Jesus used the phrase in a neutral sense to refer to himself indirectly, in the sense of our 'one', implying the limitations of his humanness. Not unlikely, he had in mind as well the 'one like a son of man' of Daniel 7:13 who had a vindication-following-suffering role. Jesus was the human one, serving God's purpose, and looking to vindication at the completion of his mission.

Early Christians embraced the phrase, now regarded as a title. There are three types of Son of Man sayings in the gospels: Those which refer to the earthly activity of the Son of Man (Mk 2:10, 28). Those which refer to the suffering Son of Man (e.g. Mk 8:31). Those which refer to the future glory and *parousia* of the Son of Man (e.g. Mk 14:62).

Torah – Torah, commonly translated 'Law', but better rendered 'instruction', 'guide of life' is, basically, the Pentateuch. For the Jew Torah (including both the written Torah and the *halakah*, 'the tradition of the elders' which adapted and extended the demands of the written law) was the full expression of God's purpose for his people. Indeed, Law and Lawgiver were practically identical. In this situation the Torah took on an absolute value, and one could concern oneself exclusively with the law. This was an attitude combated by Jesus, notably in Mk 7.

The Twelve – From his disciples Jesus chose a core group – the Twelve (Mk 6:7 parr). Their key role was symbolic. They symbolised the regathering, at the end of time, of all Israel, all twelve tribes. The brief mission of the Twelve (Mk 6:6-13) was a prophetic gesture; it symbolised the process of regathering. After a single attempt to complete the number, following the departure of Judas (Acts 1:15-26), it was evidently understood that the role of the Twelve was symbolic and pertained to the eschatological mission of Jesus. The Twelve as such played no role in the early church.

Select Bibliography

In addition to a handful of references in the text, this Bibliography is acknowledgment of my indebtedness to the work of other scholars.

GENERAL

Brown, R. E., *The Death of the Messiah*. Two vols. (New York: Doubleday, 1994).

Drury, J., *The Parables in the Gospels*. (New York: Crossroad, 1985).

Dunn, J. D. G., *Jesus Remembered. Christianity in the Making*, Vol 1. (Grand Rapids, MI: Eerdmans, 2003).

Meier, J. P., *A Marginal Jew*, Vol 1: *Rethinking the Historical Jesus*; Vol 2: *Mentor, Message, and Miracles* (New York: Doubleday, 1991, 1994).

Schneiders, S. M., *The Revelatory Text. Interpreting the New Testament as Sacred Scripture*. (San Francisco: Harper, 1991).

Stanton, G., *The Gospels and Jesus*. 2nd ed. (Oxford: OUP, 2002).

MARK

Achtemeier, P. J., *Mark*. (Philadelphia: Fortress, 1975).

Donahue, J. R., and Harrington, D. J., *The Gospel of Mark* (Collegeville, MN: Liturgical Press, 2002).

Harrington, W. J., *Mark* (Revised). (Wilmington, DE: M. Glazier, 1985).

Harrington, W. J., *Mark: Realistic Theologian. The Jesus of Mark*. (Dublin: The Columba Press, 2002).

Hengel, M., *Studies in the Gospel of Mark*. (Philadelphia: Fortress, 1985).

Hooker, M. D., *The Gospel According to St Mark*. Peabody, MA: Hendrickson, 1991).

Kingsbury, J. D., *Conflict in Mark: Jesus, Authorities, Disciples*. (Minneapolis: Fortress, 1989).

Moloney, F. J., *The Gospel of Mark. A Commentary*. (Peabody, MA: Hendrickson, 2002).

Mullins, M., *The Gospel of Mark. A Commentary.* (Dublin: The Columba Press, 2005).

Nineham, D. E., *Saint Mark.* (Baltimore: Penguin Books, 1963).

Rhoads, D. and Michie, D., *Mark as Story.* (Philadelphia: Fortress, 1982).

Schweizer, E., *The Good News According to Mark.* (Richmond. VA: John Knox Press, 1970).

Senior, D., *The Passion of Jesus in the Gospel of Mark.* (Wilmington, DE: M. Glazier, 1984).

Stock, A., *The Method and Message of Mark.* (Wilmington, DE: M. Glazier, 1985).

Taylor, V., *The Gospel According to St Mark.* (London: Macmillan, 1966).

Thurson, B. B., *Preaching Mark.* (Minneapolis: Fortress, 2002).

Williamson, L., *Mark.* (Louisville: John Knox, 1983).

Interpretation 47 (1993), No. 4. *The Gospel of Mark.*